Table of Contents

Part One

OVERVIEW

Part Two

DEFINITIONS AND REPORTING PROCEDURES

Children First

National Guidelines

for the Protection and

Welfare of Children

September 1999

BAILE ÁTHA CLIATH
ARNA FHOILSIÚ AG OIFIG AN tSOLÁTHAIR
Le ceannach díreach ón
OIFIG DHÍOLTA FOILSEACHÁN RIALTAIS,
TEACH SUN ALLIANCE, SRÁID THEACH LAIGHEAN, BAILE ÁTHA CLIATH 2,
nó tríd an bpost ó
FOILSEACHÁIN RIALTAIS, AN RANNÓG POST-TRÁCHTA,
4 - 5 BÓTHAR FHEARCHAIR, BAILE ÁTHA CLIATH 2,
(Teil: 01 - 6476834/35/36/37; Fax: 01 - 4752760)
nó trí aon díoltóir leabhar.

———

DUBLIN
PUBLISHED BY THE STATIONERY OFFICE
To be purchased directly from the
GOVERNMENT PUBLICATIONS SALE OFFICE,
SUN ALLIANCE HOUSE, MOLESWORTH STREET, DUBLIN 2,
or by mail order from
GOVERNMENT PUBLICATIONS, POSTAL TRADE SECTION,
4 - 5 HARCOURT ROAD, DUBLIN 2,
(Tel: 01 - 6476834/35/36/37; Fax: 01 - 4752760)
or through any bookseller.

———

£5.00   €6.35

Wt. P65000. 70,000. 9/99. Cahill. (60642). G.Spl.

Part Three

RESPONSES OF THE HEALTH BOARD AND AN GARDA SÍOCHÁNA TO CHILD ABUSE AND CHILDREN AT RISK

Chapter Nine
An Garda Síochána-Health Board Protocol   85

Part Four

SPECIAL CONSIDERATIONS

Chapter Ten
Specially Vulnerable Children and Abuse Outside the Home   99

Part Five

LOCAL ARRANGEMENTS

Chapter Fifteen
Content and Format of Local Procedures and Guidance 121

Part Six
APPENDICES

Foreword by the Minister of State with Special Responsibility for Children

In recent years as a society, we have become very aware of the problem of child abuse. This period has also seen a major investment in child care and family support services to enable health boards to respond to child abuse and welfare concerns. The production of "Children First", the national child protection guidelines, is a further important step in strengthening arrangements for the protection of children. Revised guidelines were urgently needed and "Children First" will help organisations of all types and sizes to improve their policies, procedures and practices to safeguard children and young people. They are informative and user-friendly and based on the key principle that the best interests of the child are paramount.

One important point is that everyone has a duty to protect children and that this is not simply the job of social workers and other health professionals. The Government has decided that "Children First" should be national guidelines which are applied consistently by health boards, Government Departments and by organisations which provide services to children. They are intended, in particular, to support and guide health professionals, teachers, members of the Garda Síochána and the many people in sporting, cultural, community and voluntary organisations who come into regular contact with children and are therefore in a position of responsibility in recognising and responding to possible child abuse. I am confident that they will achieve the objective of encouraging and helping people to report child abuse concerns. In this regard, the enactment of the Protections for Persons Reporting Child Abuse Act 1998 which provides a statutory immunity for persons reporting child abuse "reasonably and in good faith" is another milestone.

I appreciate that child protection work is complex, uncertain and unpredictable. "Children First" provides professionals with a set of sound principles and good practice guidelines. They emphasise the importance of inter-agency co-operation and outline the various steps to be followed in order to protect children at risk and try to prevent the recurrence of child abuse.

The Government is committed to the full implementation of "Children First". The national guidelines will be made widely available and this will be linked to a public information campaign. In addition, resources are being provided for a programme of training in child protection and the use of the guidelines.

Finally, I would like to thank the members of the Working Group for their dedication and persistence in bringing this project to a successful conclusion and to convey my appreciation to all the individuals and organisations who contributed to the preparation of "Children First".

Frank Fahey T.D.
Minister of State with Special Responsibility for Children
September 1999

Preface

Terms of Reference

In February, 1998, Mr. Frank Fahey TD, Minister of State at the Department of Health and Children established a **"WORKING GROUP TO REVIEW THE CHILD ABUSE GUIDELINES"**.

The Terms of Reference of the Working Group were as follows:
"In view of the implementation of the Child Care Act, 1991, changes in the management of health boards and the commitment of the Government to introduce mandatory reporting of child abuse to review

(i) Guidelines on procedures for the identification, investigation and management of child abuse and

(ii) Notification of Suspected Cases of Child Abuse between Health Boards and Gardaí

and to prepare revised guidelines aimed at improving the identification, investigation and management of child abuse."

Membership

The Minister of State appointed to the Working Group an independent Chair and representatives of a wide range of the key interests involved. The members of the Working Group were:

Maureen P Lynott, Director of Provider Affairs, BUPA Ireland Ltd., (Chair).

Mary Bennett, Chair, Irish Society for the Prevention of Cruelty to Children.

Olive Braiden, Director, Dublin Rape Crisis Centre.

Dr Helen Buckley, Lecturer, Department of Social Studies, Trinity College Dublin.

Christina Carney, Assistant General Secretary, Irish Municipal, Public and Civil Trade Union.

John Carr, General Treasurer, Irish National Teachers Organisation.

Brid Clarke, Programme Manager, Children and Families, Eastern Health Board.

Madeleine Clarke, Chairperson, Children's Rights Alliance.

Dr Brian Coffey, Chairman, Irish College of General Practitioners.

Patrick Cregg, Chief Superintendent, An Garda Síochána.*

Ger Crowley, A/Assistant Chief Executive Officer, Mid-Western Health Board.

---

* Chief Superintendent O'Sullivan resigned from the Group on transfer in June, 1998 and was replaced by Chief Superintendent Cregg who was assisted by Inspector Karl Heller.

Mary Curran, Superintendent Public Health Nurse, North-Western Health Board.

Michael Flanagan, Divisional Inspector, Department of Education and Science.

Dr David Lillis, President, Irish Hospital Consultants Association.

Jimmy Martin, Principal Officer, Garda Division, Department of Justice, Equality and Law Reform.

Augusta McCabe, Social Worker Adviser, Child Care Policy Unit, Department of Health and Children.

Dr Kevin McCoy, Chief Inspector, Northern Ireland Social Services Inspectorate.

Noel O'Sullivan, Chief Superintendent, An Garda Síochána*.

Bernie Price, Head Medical Social Worker, Medical Social Work Department, The Children's Hospital, Temple Street.

Frances Spillane, Principal Officer, Child Care Legislation Unit, Department of Health and Children.

Dermot Ryan, Assistant Principal Officer, Child Care Legislation Unit, Department of Health and Children (Secretary).

Approach of the Working Group

The Working Group met for the first time on 3rd March, 1998 and had a further sixteen meetings.

In preparing these new National Guidelines, the Working Group reviewed practice in health boards and non-statutory organisations, as well as the findings of major inquiry reports into specific child abuse cases. The Working Group obtained comprehensive input from health boards, non-statutory groups and individuals. A key finding in the Working Group's deliberations was the significant variation in how organisations operate child protection procedures and arrangements. Past experience and practice has significantly informed the National Guidelines and the Working Group's recommendations for their implementation.

The Working Group have recommended and emphasised:

- the need for consistent application of the National Guidelines

- the need for comprehensive training

- the importance of support services to children and families

- the clear designation of responsibility and roles in child protection

- the essential requirement of co-operative inter-agency and multi-disciplinary working.
The National Guidelines are intended:

- to improve the ability of staff who work with children to recognise child abuse and to be aware of child protection procedures and practices;

---

* Chief Superintendent O'Sullivan resigned from the Group on transfer in June, 1998 and was replaced by Chief Superintendent Cregg who was assisted by Inspector Karl Heller.

- to provide health board personnel with clear guidance in assessing child abuse cases;
- to support and encourage organisations to work co-operatively in protecting children.

It is the firm view of the Working Group that individuals must primarily be responsible for the reporting of concerns or suspicions of child abuse. The Working Group wish to emphasise that it is the health board's responsibility to assess child protection concerns. However, an individual, whether in an organisation or part of the community, has a responsibility to report concerns or suspicions to the health boards. The National Guidelines also call for specific procedures for corporate organisational responsibility, appropriate staff training and designation of specific personnel to liaise with the health boards in regard to concerns or suspicions of child abuse.

Submissions and Consultations

The Working Group wishes to express its gratitude to the many individuals and organisations who responded to its invitation to make written submission to the Working Group. Their contributions were fully examined and much appreciated. The Working Group also invited a number of individuals and organisations to meet with them to discuss particular aspects of their brief. We are grateful to them for their help and co-operation and for the expert insights which they afforded us.

Appreciation

We are deeply indebted to our Secretary, Dermot Ryan, for all he contributed throughout the work of the Working Group and in the preparation of the National Guidelines. His efficiency and thoroughness at all times deserve the highest commendation. We would also wish to record our appreciation of the contribution of Brendan Coogan, Administrative Officer, for all of his support and dedication during his time with the Working Group from February 1998 until March 1999.

Maureen Lynott
Chair
June 1999*

---

*   Following submission of the report to the Minister of State in June 1999, a legal review of the Guidelines was completed by the Attorney General's Office which necessitated a number of amendments to the Working Group's draft. The final draft was then submitted to the Government and approved on 26th July 1999.

Overview

part one

1 Principles, Aims and Use of These Guidelines

1.1 Introduction

1.1.1 Since the publication of the 1987 Child Abuse Guidelines by the Department of Health, the profile of child abuse as a social problem has risen considerably in Ireland. During this period, significant reforms have taken place in terms of legislation, policies and services established to promote the protection and welfare of children. The Child Care Act, 1991 updated legislation for the welfare and protection of children. In September 1992, the UN Convention on the Rights of the Child was ratified by Ireland and came into force on 21 October 1992. Health board community care services have been expanded considerably and management responsibilities for child care and child protection have been re-organised.

1.1.2 A number of major inquiries have taken place into cases of serious child abuse. The findings and recommendations emanating from these have informed and shaped current child protection policy and procedures. Research has been undertaken and academic programmes in child protection and welfare have been put in place. These activities are contributing to an increased focus on best professional practice, with an emphasis on the importance of inter-professional and inter-agency co-ordination and co-operation.

1.2 Aim of the National Guidelines

1.2.1 These National Guidelines are intended to assist people in identifying and reporting child abuse. They aim, in particular, to clarify and promote mutual understanding among statutory and voluntary organisations about the contributions of different disciplines and professions to child protection. They emphasise that the needs of children and families must be at the centre of child care and child protection activity and that a partnership approach must inform the delivery of services. They also highlight the importance of consistency between policies and procedures across health boards and other statutory and voluntary organisations. They emphasise in particular that the welfare of children is of paramount importance.

1.2.2 The National Guidelines cover all children and not just children who are victims of abuse or neglect. Inevitably, the investigation of child abuse involves an intrusion of privacy but this is offset by the greater good of protecting the child and other potential victims in the community; it is also offset by the need to honour legal and constitutional imperatives to punish the criminal abuser. One of the primary considerations of these National Guidelines is to minimise the stress involved by the investigation and assessment of child abuse.

1.3 Use of the National Guidelines

1.3.1 These are National Guidelines. They are directed at a wide audience of individuals and agencies who have contact with or provide services for children. Part Three of the National Guidelines is aimed specifically at health boards and An Garda Síochána, which are the two agencies with statutory responsibility for child protection.

1.3.2 These National Guidelines must be complemented at a local level by regional health board procedures and guidance which is specific to particular disciplines or organisations in order to maximise their usefulness and relevance to staff. Any such guidance must adopt the basic aims and objectives outlined in this document. Chapter Fifteen indicates how this should be done.

1.3.3 Each organisation should designate responsibility to a specific member of staff for ensuring that procedures and arrangements are in place within the organisation to protect children in line with these National Guidelines.

1.3.4 These National Guidelines are intended to provide a framework for inter-agency and multi-professional work practices. They are based on specific principles and responsibilities in order to ensure that the needs of children who are abused or at risk of abuse are adequately addressed. However, effective child protection will only be achieved in a context where these National Guidelines and local procedures are supported by comprehensive training, supervision, adequate resources, and support services for families and children.

1.3.5 As stated above, the National Guidelines are directed at a wide audience of individuals and agencies who have contact with children and the main aim of the National Guidelines is to assist people in identifying and reporting child abuse. At present there is voluntary reporting of child abuse in Ireland. Society has a duty of care towards children and everyone should be alert to the possibility that children with whom they are in contact may be being abused. It is hoped that these National Guidelines will encourage people to report concerns or suspicions to the health boards in particular through education of professionals, voluntary and community groups about child abuse and development of local or organisational procedures.

1.3.6 These National Guidelines are directed at health board personnel, An Garda Síochána, other public agencies, voluntary and community organisations and private citizens. In the case of the health boards, the National Guidelines are being issued in the context of the Child Care Act, 1991. In the case of other agencies and individuals, while the National Guidelines do not have a legislative background, the intention is the development of good practice in this important area of public policy. The successful operation of the National Guidelines will be dependent on the goodwill, support and co-operation of all members of the community.

1.4   Objectives

1.4.1   The objectives of these National Guidelines may be summarised as follows:

(i) They should improve the identification, reporting, assessment, treatment and management of child abuse.

(ii) Having regard to the findings from official child abuse inquiries carried out in Ireland, the National Guidelines should facilitate effective child protection work by emphasising the importance of family support services and the need for clarity of responsibility between various professional disciplines.

(iii) The National Guidelines should maximise the capacity of staff and organisations to protect children effectively by virtue of their relevance and comprehensiveness.

(iv) The National Guidelines should consolidate inter-agency co-operation based on clarity of responsibility, co-ordination of information, and partnership arrangements between disciplines and agencies.

1.5   The Child Care Act, 1991

1.5.1   The legislative basis for dealing with children in need of care and protection is provided by the Child Care Act, 1991. The promotion of the welfare of children is the paramount principle underpinning the Act. Section 3, which is the cornerstone of the Act, outlines the functions of health boards as follows:

"3.—(1) It shall be a function of every health board to promote the welfare of children in its area who are not receiving adequate care and protection.

(2) In the performance of this function, a health board shall—

(a) take such steps as it considers requisite to identify children who are not receiving adequate care and protection and co-ordinate information from all relevant sources relating to children in its area;

(b) having regard to the rights and duties of parents, whether under the Constitution or otherwise—

(i) regard the welfare of the child as the first and paramount consideration, and

(ii) in so far as is practicable, give due consideration, having regard to his age and understanding, to the wishes of the child; and

(c) have regard to the principle that it is generally in the best interests of a child be brought up in his own family.

(3) A health board shall, in addition to any other function assigned to it under this Act or any other enactment, provide child care and family support services, and may provide and maintain premises and make such other provision as it considers

necessary or desirable for such purposes, subject to any general directions given by the Minister under section 69."

1.6 The UN Convention on the Rights of the Child

1.6.1 Ireland ratified the UN Convention on the Rights of the Child in 1992. The Convention is in essence a "bill of rights" for all children. It contains rights relating to every aspect of children's lives including the right to survival, development, protection and participation. The underlying principles of the Convention may be summarised as follows:

> (i) Non-discrimination (Article 2): All rights apply to all children without exception. The State is obliged to protect children from any form of discrimination and to take positive action to promote their rights.
>
> (ii) Best Interests of the Child (Article 3): All actions concerning the child shall take account of his or her best interests. The State shall provide the child with adequate care when parents, or others charged with that responsibility fail to do so.
>
> (iii) Survival and Development (Article 6): Every child has the inherent right to life, and the State has an obligation to ensure the child's survival and development.
>
> (iv) The Child's Opinion (Article 12): The child has the right to express his or her opinion freely and to have that opinion taken into account in any matter or procedure affecting the child.

1.6.2 The Convention recognises the critical role of the family in the life of a child. It states that the family, as the fundamental group of society and the natural environment for the well-being and growth of all its members and particularly children, should be afforded the necessary protection and assistance so that it can fully assume its responsibilities in the community.

1.6.3 A number of articles of the Convention are of particular relevance to child protection.

> (i) Article 19 states that parties shall take all appropriate legislative, administrative, social and educational measures to protect the child from all forms of physical or mental violence, injury or abuse, while in the care of parent(s), legal guardian(s) or any other person who has care of the child.
>
> Such protective measures should, as appropriate, include effective procedures for the establishment of social programmes to provide necessary support for the child and for those who have the care of the child, as well as for other forms of prevention and for identification, reporting, referral, investigation, treatment and follow up of instances of child maltreatment described heretofore, and, as appropriate for judicial involvement.
>
> (ii) Articles 34 and 35 refer respectively to the protection of children from sexual exploitation and from sale, trafficking and abduction.

1.7   Policy Context

1.7.1   The enactment of the Child Care Act, 1991 is the most important policy development in recent years in the area of child care services. The Act was passed by the Oireachtas in 1991. It was brought into operation on a phased basis and was fully implemented in December 1996. The implementation of the Act was accompanied by a sustained programme of investment during the period 1993 to 1996. The provision of additional funding was continued in subsequent years so that by early 1999 a total of some IR£70 million had been provided on an ongoing basis for the development of child care and family support services.

1.7.2   The additional funding has been used to put in place a proper infrastructure for child care services, in particular the appointment of additional staff to enable the health boards to cope with their new responsibilities under the legislation. This period has seen a major increase in the number of reports of suspected child abuse to the health boards. Responding to this demand and to new responsibilities being placed on health boards under various family law acts has placed social work teams under considerable pressure.

1.7.3   At a national level, successive programmes for Government have contained commitments to the improvement of child care services. In 1994, and again in 1997, the incoming Governments appointed a Minister of State with special, cross-departmental responsibility for aspects of children's services in the areas of health, education and justice. The purpose of this appointment was to improve co-ordination of policy and services for children.

1.7.4   In 1996 the Department of Health issued a discussion document on the question of mandatory reporting of child abuse. This was followed by an extensive consultation process and the majority view was against the introduction of mandatory reporting. In early 1997, the Minister of State outlined a number of initiatives to strengthen arrangements for reporting child abuse in the document "Putting Children First — Promoting and Protecting the Rights of Children". These initiatives were:

(i) the appointment of Child Care Managers as the designated officers in the health boards to co-ordinate inter-agency approaches to child protection within each community care area;

(ii) the establishment of regional and local area child protection committees to enhance inter-agency and inter- professional approaches to child protection;

(iii) the provision of multi-disciplinary training under the aegis of the regional child protection committees;

(iv) the review of the 1987 Child Abuse Guidelines and 1995 Garda Síochána-Health Board Guidelines;

(v) the holding of a public information campaign to heighten public awareness of child abuse;

(vi) the provision of support services by health boards for victims of abuse;

(vii) the funding of voluntary agencies dealing with children to be conditional on procedures being in place to deal with allegations of child abuse;

(viii) the evaluation of the impact of these measures on the reporting of child abuse.

1.7.5 The programme for government which was launched in June 1997, entitled An Action Programme for the Millennium, contains a number of key commitments in the area of child care services including mandatory reporting of child abuse and a review of community care child protection services. The Protections for Persons Reporting Child Abuse Act was passed in December 1998 and provides a statutory immunity to persons reporting allegations of child abuse to the health boards or An Garda Síochána once they do so reasonably and in good faith.

1.8 Duty to Protect Children and Support Families

1.8.1 Children, because of their dependency and immaturity, are vulnerable to abuse in its various forms. Parents or guardians have primary responsibility for the care and protection of their children. When parents or guardians do not or cannot fulfill this responsibility, it may be necessary for health boards to intervene to ensure that children are adequately protected.

1.8.2 The wider community also has a responsibility for the welfare and protection of children. All personnel involved in organisations working with children should be alert to the possibility of child abuse. They need to be aware of their obligations to convey any reasonable concerns or suspicions to the health board and/or An Garda Síochána and to be informed of the correct procedures for doing so. The wider community of relatives, friends and neighbours are well placed to help and must also be aware of the steps to take if a concern arises. Personnel working with children and the wider public should know that early action by them is often the best way to protect children and to enable a family to stay together.

1.9 Principles for Best Practice in Child Protection

1.9.1 The principles which should inform best practice in child protection include the following:

(i) The welfare of children is of paramount importance.

(ii) A proper balance must be struck between protecting children and respecting the rights and needs of parents/carers and families; but where there is conflict, the child's welfare must come first.

(iii) Children have a right to be heard, listened to and to be taken seriously. Taking account of their age and understanding, they should be consulted and involved in all matters and decisions which may affect their lives.

(iv) Early intervention and support should be available to promote the welfare of children and families, particularly where they are vulnerable or at risk of not receiving adequate care or protection.

(v) Parents/carers have a right to respect and should be consulted and involved in matters which concern their family.

(vi) Actions taken to protect a child, including assessment, should not in themselves be abusive or cause the child unnecessary distress. Every action and procedure should consider the overall needs of the child.

(vii) Intervention should not deal with the child in isolation; the child must be seen in a family setting.

(viii) The criminal dimension of any action cannot be ignored.

(ix) Children should only be separated from parents/carers when all alternative means of protecting them have been exhausted. Re-union should always be considered.

(x) Agencies or individuals taking protective action should consider factors such as the child's gender, age, stage of development, religion, culture or race.

(xi) Effective prevention, detection and treatment of child abuse or neglect requires a co-ordinated multi- disciplinary approach to child care work and effective inter-agency management of individual cases. All agencies and disciplines concerned with the protection and welfare of children must work co-operatively in the best interests of children and their families.

(xii) In practice, effective child protection requires compulsory training and clarity of responsibility for personnel involved in organisations working with children.

2 *Key Legislative Provisions*

2.1 Purpose

2.1.1 This chapter outlines various legislative provisions relevant to child protection work. All health board staff and the personnel of voluntary and statutory agencies working with children need to be aware of their principal obligations.

2.1.2 The main legislation governing the care and protection of children is the Child Care Act, 1991. The Domestic Violence Act, 1996 and the Protections for Persons Reporting Child Abuse Act, 1998 are also relevant to child protection and welfare.

2.2 The Child Care Act, 1991

2.2.1 The purpose of the Act is to "up-date the law in relation to the care of children who have been assaulted, ill-treated, neglected or sexually abused or who are at risk." The main provisions of the Act are:

> (i) the placing of a statutory duty on health boards to promote the welfare of children who are not receiving adequate care and protection up to the age of 18;
>
> (ii) the strengthening of the powers of the health boards to provide child care and family support services;
>
> (iii) the improvement of the procedures to facilitate immediate intervention by health boards and An Garda Síochána where children are in danger;
>
> (iv) the revision of provisions to enable the courts to place children who have been assaulted, ill-treated, neglected or sexually abused or who are at risk, in the care of or under the supervision of regional health boards;
>
> (v) the introduction of arrangements for the supervision and inspection of pre-school services;
>
> (vi) the revision of provisions in relation to the registration and inspection of residential centres for children.

2.3 Domestic Violence Act, 1996

2.3.1 This Act introduced major changes in the legal remedies for domestic violence. There are two main types of remedies available:

> (i) **Safety Order**: This order prohibits a person from further violence or threats of violence. It does not oblige that person to leave the family home. If the parties

> live apart, the order prohibits the violent person from watching or being in the vicinity of the home.
>
> (ii) **Barring Order**: This order requires the violent person to leave the family home.

2.3.2 The legislation gives health boards power to intervene to protect individuals and their children from violence. Section 6 of the Act empowers health boards to apply for orders for which a person could apply on his or her own behalf but is deterred from doing so through fear or trauma. The consent of the victim is not a prerequisite for such an application, although (s)he must be consulted. Under Section 7 of the Act, the Court may, where it considers it appropriate, adjourn proceedings and direct the relevant health board to undertake an investigation of the dependent person's circumstances with a view to:

> (i) applying for a Care Order or a Supervision Order under the Child Care Act, 1991.
>
> (ii) providing services or assistance for the dependent person's family, or
>
> (iii) taking any other action in respect of the dependent person.

2.4   Protections for Persons Reporting Child Abuse Act, 1998

2.4.1 This Act came into operation on 23rd January, 1999. The main provision of the Act are:

> (i) the provision of immunity from civil liability to any person who reports child abuse "reasonably and in good faith" to designated officers of health boards or any member of An Garda Síochána.
>
> (ii) the provision of significant protections for employees who report child abuse. These protections cover all employees and all forms of discrimination up to, and including, dismissal.
>
> (iii) the creation of a new offence of false reporting of child abuse where a person makes a report of child abuse to the appropriate authorities "knowing that statement to be false". This is a new criminal offence designed to protect innocent persons from malicious reports.

2.4.2 The Chief Executive Officers of health boards have appointed a wide range of nursing, medical, paramedical and other staff as designated officers for the purposes of the Act. Section 6 of the Act is a saving provision which specifies that the statutory immunity provided under the Act for persons reporting child abuse is additional to any defences already available under any other enactment or rule of law in force immediately before the passing of the Act.

2.5   The Data Protection Act, 1988

2.5.1 The Act only applies to the automatic processing of personal data. It gives a right to every individual, irrespective of nationality or residence, to establish the existence of personal data, to have access to any such data relating to him and to have inaccurate data rectified or erased. It requires data controllers to make sure that the data they keep are collected fairly, are accurate and up-to-date, are kept for lawful purposes, and are not used or disclosed in any manner incompatible with those purposes. It also requires both data controllers and data processors to protect the data they keep, and imposes on them a special duty of care in relation to the individuals about whom they keep such data.

2.5.2   There are only three exclusions under the Act:

    (i) data relating to state security;

    (ii) information that is required by law to be made available to the public;

    (iii) personal data kept only for personal or recreational purposes.

2.6   The Education Act, 1998 (not fully implemented as of June 1999)

2.6.1   This Act places an obligation on those concerned with its implementation to give practical effect to the constitutional rights of children as they relate to education and, as far as practicable and having regard to the resources available, to make available to pupils a level and quality of education appropriate to meeting their individual needs and abilities.

2.7   The Non-Fatal Offences Against the Person Act, 1997

2.7.1   The two relevant provisions of this Act are:

    (i)   it abolishes the rule of law under which teachers were immune from criminal liability in respect of physical chastisement of pupils;

    (ii) it describes circumstances in which the use of reasonable force may be justifiable.

2.8   Freedom of Information Act, 1997

2.8.1   This Act enables members of the public to obtain access, to the greatest extent possible consistent with the public interest and the right to privacy, to information in the possession of public bodies. The specific provisions of the Act include the following:

    (i)   to provide for a right of access to records held by such bodies, for necessary exceptions to that right and for assistance to persons to enable them to exercise it;

    (ii) to enable persons to have corrected any personal information relating to them in the possession of such bodies;

    (iii) to provide for independent review by an Information Commissioner both of decisions of such bodies relating to that right and of the operation of the Act generally;

    (iv) to provide for the publication by public bodies of guides to their functions and National Guidelines such as these for assistance of the public.

2.8.2 Under the Act, a person about whom a pubic body holds personal information has:

    (i) right of access to this information subject to certain conditions;

    (ii) right to correct this information if it is inaccurate.

2.8.3 Where a public body makes a decision which affects an individual, that person has a right to relevant reasons and findings on the part of the body reaching that decision.

2.8.4 The Act is also designed to protect the privacy of individuals and, in general, requires the prior consent of an individual before releasing personal information about them. Where the release of social work or medical records contains information that would be harmful to a person's well-being, the release may be made to a health professional who acts on the person's behalf. Under the Act, there are regulations and guidelines relating to access by parents to their children's records; these emphasise that the over-riding concern is the best interests of the child.

2.8.5 The exemptions and exclusions which are relevant to child protection include the following:

    (i) protecting records covered by legal professional privilege;

    (ii) protecting records which would facilitate the commission of a crime;

    (iii) protecting records which would reveal a confidential source of information.

Definitions and
Reporting Procedures

part two

3 *Definition and Recognition of Child Abuse*

3.1   Purpose

3.1.1   This chapter outlines the principal types of child abuse, and offers guidance on how to recognise it. Child abuse can be categorised into four different types: neglect, emotional abuse, physical abuse and sexual abuse. A child may be subjected to one or more forms of abuse at any given time. More details on each type of abuse is contained in **Appendix One**.

3.1.2   **In these National Guidelines "child" means a person under the age of 18 years, excluding a person who is or has been married.**

3.2   Definition of Neglect

3.2.1   Neglect can be defined in terms of an *omission*, where the child suffers significant harm or impairment of development by being deprived of food, clothing, warmth, hygiene, intellectual stimulation, supervision and safety, attachment to and affection from adults, medical care.

3.2.2   *Harm* can be defined as the ill-treatment or the impairment of the health or development of a child. Whether it is *significant* is determined by his/her health and development as compared to that which could reasonably be expected of a child of similar age.

3.2.3   Neglect generally becomes apparent in different ways *over a period of time* rather than at one specific point. For instance, a child who suffers a series of minor injuries is not having his or her needs met for supervision and safety. A child whose ongoing failure to gain weight or whose height is significantly below average may be being deprived of adequate nutrition. A child who consistently misses school may be being deprived of intellectual stimulation. The *threshold of significant harm* is reached when the child's needs are neglected to the extent that his or her well-being and/or development are severely affected.

3.3   Definition of Emotional Abuse

3.3.1   Emotional abuse is normally to be found in the *relationship* between a care-giver and a child rather than in a specific event or pattern of events. It occurs when a child's need for affection, approval, consistency and security are not met. Unless other forms of abuse are present, it is rarely manifested in terms of physical signs or symptoms. Examples of emotional abuse of children include:

(i) the imposition of negative attributes on children, expressed by persistent criticism, sarcasm, hostility or blaming;

(ii) conditional parenting in which the level of care shown to a child is made contingent on his or her behaviours or actions;

(iii) emotional unavailability by the child's parent/carer;

(iv) unresponsiveness, inconsistent, or inappropriate expectations of the child;

(v) premature imposition of responsibility on the child;

(vi) unrealistic or inappropriate expectations of the child's capacity to understand something or to behave and control himself in a certain way;

(vii) Under or over-protection of the child;

(viii) Failure to show interest in, or provide age-appropriate opportunities for, the child's cognitive and emotional development;

(ix) use of unreasonable or over-harsh disciplinary measures;

(x) exposure to domestic violence.

3.3.2 Emotional abuse can be manifested in terms of the child's behavioural, cognitive, affective or physical functioning. Examples of these include: 'anxious' attachment, non-organic failure to thrive, unhappiness, low self-esteem, educational and developmental underachievement, and oppositional behaviour. The *threshold of significant harm* is reached when abusive interactions dominate and become *typical* of the relationship between the child and the parent/carer.

3.4 Definition of Physical Abuse

3.4.1 Physical abuse is any form of non-accidental injury or injury which results from wilful or neglectful failure to protect a child. Examples of physical injury include the following:

(i) shaking

(ii) use of excessive force in handling (iii) deliberate poisoning

(iv) suffocation

(v) Munchausen's Syndrome by Proxy*

(vi) allowing or creating a substantial risk of significant harm to a child.

---

* This is a condition where parents, usually the mother (according to current research and case experience), fabricate stories of illness about their child or cause physical signs of illness. This can occur where the parent secretly administers dangerous drugs or other poisonous substances to the child or by smothering. The symptoms which alert to the possibility of Munchausen Syndrome by Proxy include the following:

  (i) symptoms which cannot be explained by any medical tests; symptoms never observed by anyone other than the carer; symptoms reported to occur only at home or when a parent visits a child in hospital;
  (ii) high level of demand for investigations of symptoms without any documented physical signs;

  (iii) unexplained problems with medical treatment such as drips coming out and lines being interfered with;

  (iv) presence of unprescribed medication or poisons in the blood or urine.

    Please refer to **Appendix One** for a more detailed analysis of patterns noted and for details of how suspected cases should be managed. Management of such cases will differ from other suspected cases of child abuse, particularly in regard to contact with parents and advising parents of concerns.

3.5 Definition of Sexual Abuse

3.5.1 Sexual abuse occurs when a child is used by another person for his or her gratification or sexual arousal or for that of others. Examples of child sexual abuse include the following:

(i) exposure of the sexual organs or any sexual act intentionally performed in the presence of the child;

(ii) intentional touching or molesting of the body of a child whether by a person or object for the purpose of sexual arousal or gratification;

(iii) masturbation in the presence of the child or the involvement of the child in an act of masturbation;

(iv) sexual intercourse with the child whether oral, vaginal, or anal;

(v) Sexual exploitation of a child includes inciting, encouraging propositioning, requiring or permitting a child to solicit for, or to engage in, prostitution or other sexual acts. Sexual exploitation also occurs when a child is involved in the exhibition, modelling or posing for the purpose of sexual arousal, gratification or sexual act, including its recording (on film, video tape or other media) or the manipulation, for those purposes, of the image by computer or other means. It may also include showing sexually explicit material to children which is often a feature of the "grooming" process by perpetrators of abuse.

(vi) Consensual sexual activity involving an adult and an under-age person. In relation to **child sexual abuse**, it should be noted that, for the purposes of the criminal law, the age of consent to sexual intercourse is 17 years. This means, for example, that sexual intercourse between a 16 year-old girl and her 17 year-old boyfriend is illegal, although it might not be regarded as constituting **child sexual abuse**.

The decision to initiate child protection action in such cases is a matter for professional judgement and each case should be considered individually. The criminal aspects of the case, will be dealt with by An Garda Síochána under the relevant legislation.

It should be noted that the definition of child sexual abuse presented in this section is not a legal definition and is not intended to be a description of the criminal offences of sexual assault.

3.6 Children with Special Vulnerabilities

3.6.1 Certain children are more vulnerable to abuse than others. These include children with disabilities and children who, for one reason or another, are separated from parents or other family members and who depend on others for their care and protection. The same categories of abuse — neglect, emotional abuse, physical abuse, sexual abuse — may be applicable, but may take a slightly different form. For example, abuse may take the form of deprivation of basic rights, harsh disciplinary regimes or the inappropriate use of medications or physical restraints. (See Chapter Ten below on Specially Vulnerable Children and Abuse Outside the Home).

3.7 Fatal Child Abuse

3.7.1 In the tragic circumstances where a child dies as a result of abuse or neglect there are three important facets to be considered: criminal, child protection and bereavement aspects.

3.7.2 The criminal aspects: This is the responsibility of An Garda Síochána and they must be notified immediately. The coroner must also be notified and his/her instructions must be complied with in relation to post-mortems and other relevant matters.

3.7.3 Child protection aspects: These will be particularly relevant if there are other children in the family and will require immediate health board intervention to assess risk.

3.7.4 Bereavement aspects: The bereavement needs of the family must be given priority and all family members, including the alleged abuser, if a family member, should be given an opportunity to grieve and say goodbye to the dead child. Hospital staff are well placed to facilitate this.

3.8 Recognising Child Abuse

3.8.1 Child abuse can often be difficult to identify and may present in many forms. Early detection is important and professionals working with children should share their concerns about child protection or welfare with colleagues, preferably those in senior line management positions.

3.8.2 A list of child abuse indicators is contained in **Appendix Two**. It is important to stress that no one indicator should be seen as conclusive in itself of abuse; it may indeed indicate conditions other than child abuse. All signs and symptoms must be examined in the total context of the child's situation and family circumstances.

3.9 Guidelines for Recognition

3.9.1 The ability to recognise child abuse depends as much on a person's willingness to accept the possibility of its existence as it does on their knowledge and information. There are commonly three stages in the identification of child abuse. These are:

> (i) considering the possibility
>
> (ii) looking out for signs of abuse
>
> (iii) recording of information

Stage One: Considering the Possibility

3.9.2 The possibility of child abuse should be considered if a child appears to have suffered a suspicious injury for which no reasonable explanation can be offered. It should also be considered if the child seems distressed without obvious reason or displays persistent or new behavioural problems. The possibility of child abuse should also be considered if the child displays unusual or fearful responses to parents/ carers.

Stage Two: Looking out for Signs of Abuse

3.9.3 Signs of abuse can be physical, behavioural, or developmental. They can exist in the relationships between children and parents/ carers or between children and other family members. A cluster or pattern of signs is likely to be more indicative of abuse. Children who are being abused may hint that they are being harmed and sometimes make direct disclosures. Disclosures should always be believed; less obvious signs could be gently explored with the child, *without direct questioning*. Play situations such as drawing or story telling may reveal information.

3.9.4 Some signs are more indicative of abuse than others. These include:

>   (i) disclosure of abuse and neglect by a child or young person;
>
>   (ii) age-inappropriate or abnormal sexual play or knowledge;
>
>   (iii) specific injuries or patterns of injuries;
>
>   (iv) absconding from home or a care situation;
>
>   (v) attempted suicide;
>
>   (vi) under-age pregnancy or sexually transmitted disease;
>
>   (vii) signs in one or more categories at the same time. For example, signs of developmental delay, physical injury and behavioural signs may together indicate a pattern of abuse.

3.9.5 Most signs are non-specific and must be considered in the child's social and family context. It is important to always be open to alternative explanations for physical or behavioural signs of abuse. Sometimes, a specialist assessment may be required to clarify if particular concerns constitute abuse.

Stage Three: Recording of Information

3.9.6 If abuse is suspected, it is important to establish the grounds for concern by obtaining as much detailed information as possible. Observations should be accurately recorded and should include dates, times, names, locations, context and any other information which may be relevant.

3.10 Points to Remember

3.10.1 **The severity of a sign does not necessarily equate with the severity of the abuse.** Severe and potentially fatal injuries are not always visible. Emotional and/or psychological abuse tends to be cumulative and effects may only be observable in the longer term. Signs or indicators of abuse should be gently explored with the child; explanations which are inconsistent with the signs should constitute a cause for concern.

3.10.2 **Neglect is as potentially fatal as physical abuse.** It can cause delayed physical, psychological and emotional development, chronic ill-health and significant long-term damage. It may also precede, or co-exist with, other forms of abuse and must be treated seriously.

3.10.3 **Child abuse is not restricted to any socio-economic group, gender or culture.** All signs must be considered in the wider social and family context. However serious deficits in child safety and welfare transcend cultural, social and ethnic norms and must elicit a response.

3.10.4 **Challenging behaviour by a child or young person should not render them liable to abuse.** Children in certain circumstances may present management problems. This should not leave them vulnerable to harsh disciplinary measures or neglect of care.

3.10.5 **It is sometimes difficult to distinguish between indicators of child abuse and other adversities suffered by children and families.** Deprivation, stress or mental health problems should not be used as a justification for omissions of care or commissions of harm by parents/carers. The child's welfare must be the primary consideration.

3.10.6 **The aim of child protection services is to promote positive and enduring change in the lives of children and families.** All action taken with respect to children and young people must reflect the principles and objectives of the Child Care Act, 1991. Priority must be given to the safety and well-being of the child.

3.10.7 **Society has a duty of care towards children.** Parents/carers are primarily responsible for the safety and welfare of the children in their care. The health board is the statutory body responsible for child protection and welfare and must intervene when children are harmed or fail to receive adequate care. However, health board professionals are dependent on the co-operation of members of the public and professionals in contact with children to bring child care and protection concerns to their attention in as comprehensive a fashion as possible.

4 Basis For Reporting and Standard Reporting Procedure

4.1 Purpose

4.1.1 This chapter offers guidance to the general public and to persons working with children who may be concerned or who suspect that children are being harmed or at risk of harm. It outlines the standard reporting procedure to be used in passing information to the statutory authorities about child protection concerns.

4.2 Responsibility to Report Child Abuse

4.2.1 Everyone must be alert to the possibility that children with whom they are in contact may be being abused. Concerns should be reported to the health board. This responsibility is particularly relevant to professionals such as teachers, child care workers and health professionals who have regular contact with children in the course of their work. It is also an important responsibility for staff and volunteers involved in sports clubs, parish activities, youth clubs and other organisations catering for children.

4.2.2 The guiding principles in regard to reporting child abuse may be summarised as follows:

> (i) The safety and well-being of the child or young person must take priority.
>
> (ii) Reports should be made without delay to the health board.
>
> (iii) While the basis for concern must be established as comprehensively as possible, children or parents should not be interviewed in detail about the suspected abuse.

4.2.3 Any reasonable suspicion of abuse must elicit a response. Ignoring the signals or failing to intervene may result in ongoing or further harm to the child or young person. Children and young people may suffer long-lasting emotional and/or psychological harm as a result of neglect, emotional abuse or sexual abuse. Physical abuse and neglect can be fatal, and some children may be permanently disabled or disfigured as a result of child abuse.

4.2.4 If a person has misgivings about the safety of a child and would find it helpful to discuss their concerns with a professional, they should not hesitate to contact someone in the health board such as a social worker, public health nurse or staff in a health centre to discuss the matter. This should help them to decide whether or not to formally report their concerns to the health board.

4.3 Basis for Reporting to a Health Board

4.3.1 A health board should always be informed when a person has reasonable grounds for concern that a child may have been abused, or is being abused, or is at risk of abuse.

4.3.2 The following examples would constitute reasonable grounds for concern:

> (i) specific indication from the child that (s)he was abused;
>
> (ii) an account by a person who saw the child being abused;
>
> (iii) evidence, *such as an injury or behaviour* which is consistent with abuse and unlikely to be caused another way;
>
> (iv) an injury or behaviour which is consistent both with abuse and with an innocent explanation but where there are corroborative indicators supporting the concern that it may be a case of abuse. An example of this would be a pattern of injuries, an implausible explanation, other indications of abuse, dysfunctional behaviour;
>
> (v) consistent indication, over a period of time, that a child is suffering from emotional or physical neglect.

4.3.3 **A suspicion which is not supported by any objective indication of abuse or neglect would not constitute a reasonable suspicion or reasonable grounds for concern.**

4.3.4 It is important that persons reporting suspected child abuse to the health board should establish the basis for their concerns. At the same time, they should not interview the child or the child's parents/carers in any detail about the alleged abuse without first consulting the health board; this may be more appropriately carried out by the health board social worker or An Garda Síochána.

4.4 Standard Reporting Procedure

4.4.1 If child abuse is suspected or alleged, the following steps should be taken by members of the public or professionals who come into contact with children:

> (i) A report should be made to the health board in person, by phone or in writing. Each health board area has a social worker on duty for a certain number of hours each day. The duty social worker is available to meet with, or talk on the telephone, to persons wishing to report child protection concerns. (There is a list of contact numbers in **Appendix Three**).
>
> (ii) It is generally most helpful if persons wishing to report child abuse concerns make personal contact with the duty social worker. This will facilitate the social worker in gathering as much information as possible about the child and his or her parents/carers.
>
> (iii) **In the event of an emergency, or the non availability of health board staff, the report should be made to An Garda Síochána. This may be done at any Garda Station.**

NOTE: A suggested template for a Standard Reporting Form is at Appendix 4. This is for use by staff and volunteers in organisations which work with children or who are in contact with children. If a report is made by phone, this form should be forwarded subsequently to the health board.

4.5 Information Required when a Report is Being Made

4.5.1 The ability of the health board and/or An Garda Síochána to assess suspicions or allegations of child abuse will depend on the amount and quality of information conveyed to them by persons reporting their concerns. **As much as possible of the following detail should be given in the Standard Reporting Form or by telephone:**

(i) accurate identifying information as far as it is known. This should include the names, addresses and ages of the child and all children in the family as well as the parents'/ carers' names and address;

(ii) name and address of the person alleged to be causing harm to the child;

(iii) a full account of what constitutes the grounds for concern about the welfare and protection of the child or children;

(iv) source of any information which is being discussed with the health board;

(v) dates when the concern arose, or a particular incident occurred;

(vi) circumstances in which the concern arose, or the incident occurred;

(vii) any explanation offered to account for the risk, injury or concern;

(viii) the child's own statement, if relevant;

(ix) any other information regarding difficulties which the family may be experiencing. These may include illness, recent bereavement or separation, financial situation, addiction, disability, mental health problem;

(x) any factors which may be considered supportive or protective of the family. These may include helpful family members, neighbours, useful services or projects with whom they have contact;

(xi) name of child or children's school;

(xii) name of child and/or family's general practitioner;

(xiii) the reporter's own involvement with the child and parents/carers;

(xiv) details of any action already taken about the risk or concern;

(xv) names and addresses of any agencies or key persons involved with the parents/carers;

(xvi) identity of reporters including name, address, telephone number, occupation, and relationship with the family.

4.5.2 Any **professional** who suspects child abuse should inform the parents/carers if a report is to be submitted to the health board or An Garda Síochána unless doing so is likely to endanger the child.

4.5.3 In cases of emergency, where a child appears to be at immediate and serious risk, and a duty social worker is unavailable, An Garda Síochána should be contacted. **Under no circumstances should a child be left in a dangerous situation pending health board intervention.**

4.6   Retrospective Disclosures by Adults

4.6.1 In recent years there have been increasing numbers of disclosures by adults of abuse which took place during their childhood. These revelations often come to light in the context of the adults attending counselling. In these situations it is essential that consideration is given to the current risk to any child who may be in contact with the alleged abuser. If any risk is deemed to exist, the counsellor/health professional should report the allegation to the health board without delay. Investigation of disclosures by adult victims of past abuse frequently uncovers current incidences of abuse and is therefore an effective means of stopping the cycle of abuse.

4.7   Common Impediments to the Reporting of Child Abuse

4.7.1   Child abuse is a difficult and, to some people, distasteful subject. There is a common tendency to believe that it happens only to "other people". The identification of child abuse is frequently linked to personal experiences, values and beliefs, and there may be a reluctance to acknowledge its existence. The belief that parents or other persons in charge of children would actually hurt or neglect them is not easy to sustain. It is easy, therefore, to deny, minimise or explain away any signs that a child is being harmed, even when evidence exists. At times, it is hard to distinguish between abusive situations and those where other social problems such as unemployment, poverty, poor housing, mental illness or isolation are present. Sympathy for families in difficult circumstances can sometimes dilute personal or professional concerns about the safety and welfare of children.

4.7.2   Reluctance to act on suspicions about child abuse can often stem from uncertainty and fear. Members of the public or professionals may be afraid of repercussions, afraid of being thought insensitive, afraid of breaking confidence, or afraid of being disloyal. Knowledge and information about child abuse will help to overcome reluctance to take action; so too will confidence in the child protection services.

4.7.3   The *Protections for Persons Reporting Child Abuse Act, 1998* provides immunity from civil liability to persons who report child abuse "reasonably and in good faith" to designated officers* of health boards or any member of An Garda Síochána. This means that, even if a reported suspicion of child abuse proves unfounded, a plaintiff who took an action would have to prove that the reporter had not acted reasonably and in good faith in making the report.

---

*   In accordance with the power granted to him under Section 2, subsection (2) of the Act, the Minister has directed (January 1999) that the Chief Executive Officer of each health board should appoint as designated officers each person falling within the following categories of officer of the health board:

>   Social Workers
>   Child Care Workers
>   Public Health Nurses
>   Hospital Consultants
>   Psychiatrists
>   Non-Consultant Hospital Doctors
>   All other health board medical and dental personnel
>   Community Welfare Officers
>   Speech and Language Therapists
>   All health board nursing personnel
>   Psychologists
>   Radiographers
>   Physiotherapists
>   Occupational Therapists
>   Health Education Officers
>   Substance Abuse Counsellors
>   Care Assistants.

---

5 *Confidentiality, Exchange of Information & Participation of Parents/Carers*

5.1 Purpose

5.1.1 The purpose of this chapter is to give guidance on issues concerning confidentiality and the exchange of information. The effective protection of a child often depends on the willingness of the staff in statutory and voluntary organisations involved with children to share and exchange relevant information; it is critical that there is a clear understanding of professional and legal responsibilities in regard to confidentiality and exchange of information

5.1.2 The chapter also gives guidance to professionals on the positive involvement of parents/carers. The Child Care Act, 1991 enshrines *"the principle that it is generally in the best interest of a child to be brought up in his own family"*. This principle must be taken into account by the health board in promoting the welfare of children who are not receiving adequate care and protection.

5.2 Confidentiality

5.2.1 All information regarding concern or assessment of child abuse should be shared on "a need to know" basis in the interests of the child.

5.2.2 No undertakings regarding secrecy can be given. Those working with a child and family should make this clear to all parties involved.

5.2.3 Ethical and statutory codes concerned with confidentiality and data protection provide general guidance. They are not intended to limit or prevent the exchange of information between different professional staff who have a responsibility for ensuring the protection of children. **Giving information to others for the protection of a child is not a breach of confidentiality.**

5.2.4 It must be clearly understood that information which is gathered for one purpose must not be used for another without consulting the person who provided that information.

5.2.5 The issue of confidentiality should be part of the training necessary for staff who work in the area of child protection and the general training of staff in organisations which work with children. Each organisation should have a written policy in this regard.

5.3 Exchange of Information

5.3.1 Arrangements for child protection can only be successful if staff in the statutory and voluntary organisations concerned work in partnership and share relevant information, in particular with health boards and An Garda Síochána.

5.3.2 Health boards have a statutory obligation to identify children who are not receiving adequate care and protection, to provide family support services and where necessary to take children into care. People who report concerns to health board staff need to be assured that they will not automatically trigger inappropriate child protection investigations. It should be made clear that the health board will undertake a careful consideration of all the issues.

5.3.3 Anyone who receives information from colleagues about possible or actual child abuse must treat it as having been given in confidence.

5.3.4 Clear guidelines should be in place for the transfer of relevant records relating to child protection cases when a child is moved to another health board area or outside the jurisdiction. Particular reference should be made to the transfer of information/records to Northern Ireland in view of the special arrangement which now exists between the two jurisdictions, as detailed in **Appendix Nine**.

5.4   Co-operation with Parents/Carers

5.4.1 Parents/carers need to be informed of the reasons for professional concern, the statutory powers, duties and roles of the agencies, their own legal rights and any changes in the family's situation which the agencies consider necessary in the interests of the child.

5.4.2 There are four reasons why it is necessary to work in co-operation with parents/carers:

> **(i) Effectiveness**: Co-operation with families is essential to ensure the welfare of the child. It is more likely to be achieved if parents/carers are encouraged from the outset to participate in decision-making about the protection of their child/children.
>
> **(ii) Families as a Source of Information:** Family and extended family members have unique knowledge and understanding of the child's situation. This means that they can contribute to discussions about what has or has not happened to the child and the best way to provide protection.
>
> **(iii) Rights:** Family members may have rights to know what is said about them and to contribute to important decisions about their lives and those of their children. The consequences of their child's name being notified to the health board or An Garda Síochána because of a need for protection are such that parents and children should be given a proper opportunity to put their views to those who make this decision.
>
> **(iv) Empowerment:** Involvement in decision-making helps parents/carers to build up their self-esteem and encourage them to feel more in control of their lives. This should have a beneficial effect on the well being of both parents/carers and the child.

5.4.3 In addition to these reasons, it is necessary for professionals to build a foundation of understanding between themselves and parents/carers. This requires openness, honesty and the ability of professional staff to use authority appropriately. At an early stage, parents/carers and older children should be involved and given information such as leaflets and/or videos about child protection procedures. Area Child Protection Committees should pay full regard to this.

5.4.4 Parents/carers should generally be informed or consulted at every stage of an investigation/assessment. Parents'/carers' views should be sought on the issues to be raised at a child protection conference so that they can get advice and prepare their representations.

5.4.5 All actions in response to concerns about child abuse should be taken in a manner which supports the possibility of families providing safe and nurturing care for their children, now or in the future.

5.5 Perspective of Parents/Carers in Child Protection Investigations/ Assessments

5.5.1 For parents, being asked to participate in, or co-operate with, an investigation into suspected child abuse can provoke powerful emotions such as anger, fear, shame, guilt or powerlessness. Moreover, parents are usually unaware of the complexity of what is likely to be involved and are unsure of the appropriate rules of behaviour.

5.5.2 Professionals need to build trust with families when involved in child abuse investigations/assessments, in so far as is possible. It may be unrealistic to expect family members who are the subject of allegations into child abuse and neglect to trust the professionals making the enquiries. Being cast into the role of the accused inhibits parents from trying to understand the professional's point of view. Nevertheless, in many cases a relationship of trust can be established if the right conditions for its development are created by the professionals involved.

5.6 Children and Parents with Communication Difficulties

5.6.1 If the child or parent has a communication difficulty, arrangements must be made to help them during interview. This may involve a sign language interpreter, large print, tape or braille. For those whose first language is not English the use of an interpreter must be considered.

5.6.2 The need for good record-keeping at all stages of the child protection process cannot be over-emphasised. Every agency must have a policy on record-keeping and this should give all children and parents/carers access to records.

5.7 Conflict between Parents and Children

5.7.1 **Where the interests of the parents and child appear to conflict, the child's interests should be paramount.** Sometimes it may be necessary to provide a separate worker specifically for the parent; for example, it may be necessary if one of the parents is the alleged abuser.

5.8   Unfounded Allegations

5.8.1   As a consequence of raising concerns about child abuse with parents, family privacy and thus a sense of identity can be eroded. The stigma associated with social service interventions by health boards is well documented. When an assessment concludes that an allegation or suspicion is unfounded, health board staff may still need to extend support to families. Appropriate counselling services may be required.

6 Joint Working and Co-operation: Roles and Responsibilities of Agencies and Personnel Working with Children

6.1 Purpose

6.1.1 The health board has overall responsibility for the assessment and management of child protection concerns. At the same time, An Garda Síochána has responsibility for the investigation of alleged offences. No one professional has all the skills, knowledge, or resources necessary to comprehensively meet all the requirements of an individual case. It is essential therefore that a co-ordinated response is made by all professionals involved with a child and his or her carer/s. This chapter identifies the elements of effective inter-agency co-operation. It outlines the roles and responsibilities of the health board and other organisations working with children.

6.2 Inter-Agency Co-operation

6.2.1 Effective inter-agency co-operation has three benefits:

(i) It ensures provision of a comprehensive response to all concerns about children. This includes the pooling of resources and skills at all stages of intervention from initial enquiry to assessment and case management, including early identification and prevention.

(ii) It avoids gaps in the service response especially in cases where information might otherwise remain concealed or unknown.

(iii) It provides mutual support for professionals in complex cases.

6.2.2 The effectiveness and usefulness of inter-agency and inter-professional co-operation and co-ordination is influenced by certain conditions which should be addressed specifically in training programmes. These conditions include the following:

(i) dissemination on a regular basis of procedures, guidelines and policies;

(ii) clear contractual arrangements between statutory and voluntary agencies;

(iii) an understanding and acceptance by all professionals working with children of their responsibilities and roles in the promotion of child welfare;

(iv) mutual trust in the sharing of information;

(v) agreement on common goals with regard to a child's safety and welfare;

(vi) willingness of professionals to respect the contributions made by each other, irrespective of status and position within agencies and organisations;

(vii) awareness of the potential for inter-professional tensions, defensiveness, prejudices, rivalries and polarity of views which may, from time to time, prevent the needs of children from taking precedence.

6.2.3 Inter-agency and inter-professional training programmes should address these conditions but agencies may be susceptible to difficulties if the following conditions exist: high staff turnover, unfilled vacancies, isolation of staff who may be based in remote areas, non-synchronous work patterns, inaccessible information systems, or inadequate managerial and supervisory structures.

6.2.4 Training to promote inter-agency and inter-professional co-operation and co-ordination should include secretarial or receptionist staff who are frequently the recipients of urgent information and have an essential role to play in communication.

6.2.5 Inter-agency co-operation is as important in the later stages of child protection work as it is at the outset. Efforts should be consistently made by all personnel involved in a case to remain in contact, and to communicate any relevant information to the key worker, who is normally the health board social worker.

6.2.6 It is important to note that inter-agency and inter-professional co-operation and co-ordination should never become ends in themselves; the child's safety and protection must take precedence at all times; collusion must be avoided.

6.3 Role of Central Government

6.3.1 Generally Central Government and its agencies, notably the health boards, share responsibility for securing the care and safety of children. Both should ensure that children's services reach the high standards that are required to encourage, protect and support children and to satisfy public expectations. Central Government, through the Department of Health and Children, takes responsibility for the following:

(i) providing the legislative and structural framework through which the services can be delivered;

(ii) developing national policy and guidelines in consultation with health boards and other relevant parties;

(iii) setting objectives and standards;

(iv) monitoring and inspecting services and outcomes;

(v) ensuring that the resources are available to achieve these tasks.

6.4 Roles and Responsibilities of Health Boards

6.4.1 Health boards are responsible for delivering high quality services to children in line with national objectives and standards to meet local needs.

6.4.2 Board members and officials play important and complementary roles in discharging this responsibility. Board members set the strategic direction of the board's services and determine policy and priorities for their local community within the overall objectives set by Government. Officials manage services and resources in order to achieve these policy objectives and to advise the Board on the best way forward.

6.4.3 Under the Child Care Act 1991, the health board has certain statutory obligations for the protection and welfare of children. These include the following:

> (i) It must be open to receiving information from any source about any child in its area who may not be receiving adequate care and protection.

> (ii) Having received such information, it must take active steps to identify whether the child in question is in fact receiving adequate care and protection. To this end, it must co-ordinate information from all relevant sources and make an assessment of the situation.

> (iii) Having identified a child who is not receiving adequate care and protection, the health board is under a duty to take appropriate action to promote the welfare of the child.

6.4.4 The health board fulfils its responsibilities through developing a local comprehensive child protection policy, implementing and actively promoting written procedures and practice guidance, and by providing leadership and commitment to inter-agency co-operation and training. The health board also has responsibility for:

> (i) reviewing regularly all policies and procedures for local joint working;

> (ii) resourcing child protection services in line with its child care policy;

> (iii) providing clear management structures, relevant training and supervision for all staff undertaking child protection and welfare work;

> (iv) developing and maintaining standards and a quality control system;

> (v) developing procedures which enable parents/carers, children, and other significant people to make representations, including complaints;

> (vi) publishing advice for the general public, professionals and anyone caring for a child which indicates who should be contacted if they have concerns about a child being harmed;

> (viii) developing procedures to safeguard information and ensure timely transfer of records when a child or family moves from one area to another.

6.4.5 **Child Care Manager**: Every health board has Child Care Managers to co-ordinate child protection services. Child Care Managers assist and report to the General Manager in each community care area. Some of the more important tasks of the Child Care Manager include:

(i) receiving all notifications of child abuse;

(ii) taking decisions relating to the holding of Case Conferences;

(iii) ensuring inter-agency co-operation on child protection and welfare;

(iv) ensuring inter-professional and inter-programme co-operation on child protection and welfare;

(v) being a budget holder for child care services;

(vi) overseeing staff training programmes;

(vii) negotiating service agreements with voluntary service providers.

6.4.6 **Child Protection Committees**: In the area of child protection there is a need for a close working relationship between social workers, An Garda Síochána, probation services, medical practitioners, nursing staff, teachers and other relevant professionals. Co-operation between the different agencies can be difficult to achieve. The establishment of Child Protection Committees, at both regional and community care area level (similar to the ones which already exist in Northern Ireland), will assist in the development of inter-agency and inter-professional co-operation.

6.4.7 **Regional Child Protection Committees:** Regional Child Protection Committees are being established at health board level to facilitate co-ordination on a regional basis. The regional committee will develop policies to improve inter-agency and inter-professional co-operation. The primary function of the Regional Child Protection Committees is to develop a strategic approach to child protection. Regional Child Protection Committees will issue guidance on inter-disciplinary and inter-agency procedures, review annually the child protection work in the region, develop a work plan for the coming year and produce a report to the head of each constituent agency and the Child Care Advisory Committee. Their main tasks are outlined in **Appendix Five**. Membership of the Regional Child Protection Committee will consist of representatives of health board management and professional staff, educational interests, An Garda Síochána, the probation and welfare service, the Department of Social, Community and Family Affairs, general practitioners and the voluntary child care sector.

6.4.8 **Local Child Protection Committees:** Local Child Protection Committees are being established in each community care area to foster co-operation locally and to provide a forum for the sharing of knowledge and experience on the protection of children. The functions of the Local Area Child Protection Committee are outlined in **Appendix Five**. Membership of Local Child Protection Committees at community care level will mirror the membership of the Regional Child Protection Committees to ensure local implementation of co-ordinated initiatives.

6.5 An Garda Síochána

6.5.1 The involvement of An Garda Síochána in cases of child abuse stems from their primary responsibilities to protect the community and to bring offenders to justice. Where it is suspected that a crime has been committed, An Garda Síochána will have overall responsibility for the direction of any criminal investigation. It is the function of An Garda Síochána to interview and take any statements which will form part of the criminal investigation file.

6.5.2 Although An Garda Síochána may investigate, it is the responsibility of the Director of Public Prosecutions (DPP) to decide on, and to carry out, prosecution.

6.5.3 Criminal Courts require proof **beyond reasonable doubt** that the defendant committed the offence. The burden of proof rests with the prosecution. Proceedings for child protection under the Child Care Act, 1991 take place in the civil courts which require a lesser standard of proof **on the balance of probabilities.** The DPP may decide not to prosecute a person suspected of child abuse because there is insufficient evidence to meet the standard of proof. The civil courts may decide, however, that the child needs protection from that person.

6.6 An Garda Síochána-Health Board Co-operation

6.6.1 An Garda Síochána and the child care and family support services have different functions, powers and methods of working. The specific focus of the health board is on the welfare of the child and family. The specific focus of An Garda Síochána is on the investigation of alleged offences and whether a crime has been committed. Joint working between health boards and An Garda Síochána is addressed in more detail in Chapter Nine.

6.7 Individual and Corporate Responsibilities in Reporting Child Abuse

6.7.1 There are many organisations providing services to children. Some are statutory, some are voluntary and/or not for profit organisations; others are private, for profit, organisations. Whatever the motivation or service provided, there is a moral obligation on any organisation involved with children to provide them with the highest possible standard of care in order to promote their well-being and safeguard them from harm. Organisations may also be legally responsible for their failure to provide adequate care and safeguards for the children in their care.

6.7.2 All organisations providing services to children have an overall corporate duty and responsibility to safeguard children by the following means:

(i) promoting the general welfare, health, development and safety of children;

(ii) adopting and consistently applying a safe and clearly defined method of recruiting and selecting staff and volunteers;

(iii) raising awareness within the organisation about potential risks to children's safety and welfare;

(iv) developing effective procedures for responding to accidents and complaints;

(v) developing procedures to provide specific guidance to staff and volunteers who may have reasonable grounds for concern about the safety and welfare of children involved with the organisation. These procedures should not deviate from national guidelines, but could offer further elaboration to ensure local relevance and applicability. It is the responsibility of each organisation's Board of Directors/Management to ensure such policies and procedures are in place.

(vi) identifying a designated person to act as a liaison with outside agencies and a resource person to any staff member or volunteer who has child protection concerns. The designated person is responsible for reporting allegations or suspicions of child abuse to the health boards or An Garda Síochána.

6.7.3 The Protections for Persons Reporting Child Abuse Act, 1998 makes provision for the protection from civil liability of persons who have reported child abuse "reasonably and in good faith". This protection applies to organisations as well as individuals. It is considered therefore that, in the first instance, it is organisations which employ staff or use volunteers who should assume responsibility for reporting child abuse to the appropriate authorities. Reports to health boards and An Garda Síochána should be made by the designated person, following the standard reporting procedure (see Chapter Four). Each organisation should ensure that reports are passed on as quickly as possible to the statutory authorities.

6.7.4 In those cases where the organisation decides that it should not refer concerns to the health board or An Garda Síochána, the individual staff member or volunteer who raised the concern should be given a clear written statement of the reasons why the organisation is not taking action. The staff member or volunteer should be advised that, if they remain concerned about the situation, they are free to consult with, or report to, the health board or An Garda Síochána. The provisions of the Protections for Persons Reporting Child Abuse Act, 1998 apply once they report "reasonably and in good faith".

6.8   Schools

6.8.1 Teachers are particularly well placed to observe and monitor children for signs of abuse. They are the main care givers to children outside the family context and have regular contact with children in the school setting. Teachers have a general duty of care to ensure that arrangements are in place to protect children and young people from harm. In this regard, young people need to be facilitated to develop their self-esteem, confidence, independence of thought and the necessary skills to cope with possible threats to their personal safety both within and outside the school. Boards of Management, principals and senior management teams have primary responsibility for the care and welfare of their pupils. Management arrangements within primary and post-primary schools should provide for the following:

(i) the planning, development and implementation of an effective child protection programme;

(ii) continuous monitoring and evaluation of the effectiveness of such provision;

(iii) the effective implementation of agreed reporting procedures;

(iv) the planning and implementation of appropriate staff development and training programmes.

Responsibilities of School Management

6.8.2 It is the responsibility of the Board of Management of each school to do the following:

(i) have clear procedures which teachers and other school staff must follow where they suspect, or are alerted to, possible child abuse, including where a child discloses abuse;

(ii) designate a senior member of staff to have specific responsibility for child protection. In the case of primary schools, the designated liaison person for dealing with outside agencies should be the Principal or other person designated by the Board. The Principal/designated person is responsible for ensuring that the standard reporting procedure is followed so that suspected cases of child abuse are referred promptly to the local health board or An Garda Síochána.

(iii) monitor the progress of children considered to be at risk;

(iv) contribute to the prevention of child abuse through curricular provision;

(v) promote in-service training for teachers and members of Boards of Management to ensure that they have a good working knowledge of child protection issues and procedures;

(vi) have clear written procedures in place concerning action to be taken where allegations are received against school employees.

Personal Responsibilities of School Staff

6.8.3 If a child discloses to a teacher or to other school staff alleging that (s)he is being harmed by a parent/carer or any other person, the person who receives the information should listen carefully and supportively. This applies equally where the child implies that (s)he is at risk of being harmed by a parent/carer or any other person. It also applies equally if a parent/carer or any other person discloses that (s)he has harmed or is at risk of harming a child. The child or young person should not be interviewed formally; the teacher/staff member should obtain only necessary relevant facts if and when clarification is needed. **Confidentiality must never be promised to a person making a disclosure** and the requirement to report to the health board must be explained in a supportive manner. The discussion should be recorded accurately and the record retained. The teacher or other staff member should then inform the Principal or designated person who is responsible for reporting the matter to the health board or An Garda Síochána.

6.9 Medical And Health Professionals

6.9.1 Health professionals are major contributors to child protection. They promote the welfare of children through health promotion and health surveillance programmes. They are well placed to identify and refer child protection concerns, participate in assessment, attend child protection conferences and work with the health board in planning the ongoing support of the child and family.

6.9.2 Medical examination and assessment must be carried out with sensitivity and should not add to any abuse or distress already experienced by the child.

6.10 General Practitioners

6.10.1 General practitioners (GPs) are in a good position to identify indications of abuse or signs of family stress which may point, at an early stage, to a risk of child abuse. GPs have extensive knowledge of their clients' family background which enables them to make a particular contribution to abuse prevention, child protection and the long-term support of the child and family.

6.10.2 While GPs have responsibilities to all their patients, their primary consideration should be the best interests of the child. Whenever a GP becomes concerned that a child may be at risk of, or the subject of abuse of any kind, it is essential that these concerns are discussed with the relevant health board as soon as possible.

6.10.3 GPs may need to discuss their child abuse concerns with colleagues who are experienced in working with child abuse cases where clinical uncertainty exists. GPs should therefore be aware of how to contact the relevant personnel in the health board for expert medical advice. If a GP is satisfied that there are reasonable grounds for suspecting that a child is being, or has been, abused or neglected, then (s)he should immediately inform the Child Care Manager/designate in accordance with the standard reporting procedure.

6.10.4 GPs should ensure that the primary health care team/practice staff receive appropriate training in the recognition of child abuse and in the operation of local procedures. They should have clearly defined professional support and clinical supervision.

6.11 Hospitals

6.11.1 Hospitals are in a pivotal position to identify cases where reasonable grounds for concern exist about child protection and to participate in the assessment of those concerns. These concerns should be reported to line management. Hospital staff will be able to assess a child's safety and welfare on an ongoing basis while they are in hospital. Hospitals can act in a protective and preventive manner by referring to the appropriate agencies children and families who are in need of support services.

Liaison with Health Boards

6.11.2 A co-ordinated working arrangement should be established between hospitals and child protection services in health boards for the identification of child abuse and for further interventions.

Key Issues for Hospital Staff

6.11.3 All front line staff, particularly in accident and emergency departments must be alert to indicators of actual or potential child abuse. Concerns noted by any staff should be reported to line management. A multi-disciplinary approach is essential. Medical and social histories should be obtained and accurately recorded, covering the following areas:

    (i) circumstances of the child's presentation to hospital;

    (ii) details of injuries or other signs of neglect;

    (iii) explanations offered by parents/carers and/or child;

    (iv) general demeanour of parents/carers and/or child;

    (v) family history;

    (vi) whereabouts and safety of other siblings or children in the same situation;

    (vii) whether or not the child should be admitted in order to guarantee safety.

6.11.4 It is essential that an open and honest approach is taken with parents/carers who must be given full information about the concerns which exist, any further medical or social assessments, and the intention of the hospital staff to report the concern to the health board.

6.11.5 The child must be kept fully informed of all the above developments and should be allowed an opportunity to offer his or her view. Contact between parents/carers and children should be facilitated unless it is considered that the child would be endangered by so doing. **The child's needs for emotional support from parents/carers must be carefully balanced against concerns for his or her safety.**

Medical Examinations

6.11.6 The co-operation of parents/carers should be sought for examinations and tests. If co-operation is not forthcoming, the possibility of legal action should be considered and conveyed to parents/carers (see Chapter Eight, paragraph 8.13).

Fatal Child Abuse

6.11.7 Where a child has died as a result of suspected or confirmed child abuse, the following actions must be taken:

    (i) An Garda Síochána must be notified immediately;

    (ii) the coroner must be notified;

    (iii) the protection of other children in the family must be urgently considered;

    (iv) the bereavement needs of the family must be addressed with sensitivity.

6.12   Mental Health Services

6.12.1   Psychiatrists who are treating persons with a mental health problem must also consider the welfare and safety of any children in the person's family. Where they have actual concerns these must be discussed and reported to the health board as outlined in the standard reporting procedure (see Chapter Four and **Appendix Four**).

6.12.2   Where it is considered by a psychiatric team that a parent/carer's mental health problems have implications for the safety and welfare of their children, this information must be shared with the relevant health board personnel, while taking due cognisance of the issue of confidentiality.

6.12.3   Professionals in the adult mental health services may find themselves assessing persons who have a history of harming or abusing children. In such cases, the potential risk to any children with whom this person may have contact must be considered and communicated to the health board or to any other service involved in providing treatment or other assistance to the family.

6.12.4   Where work with a family involves both the victim and the perpetrator of abuse, it is essential that it is co-ordinated and that information is shared between professionals. The child's needs must remain paramount. All decisions taken in relation to parents/carers with a mental health problem which may be of relevance to child protection, such as a decision to discharge a patient back to their family, must be communicated to the relevant health board personnel.

6.13   Child and Adolescent Psychiatry Services

6.13.1   Child and adolescent psychiatric services often work with families over a long period and are particularly well placed to identify child protection concerns. Non health board services must operate child protection procedures in line with those of the health board. It is essential that they co-ordinate their work with health boards in a manner which facilitates joint work as far as possible between the two services.

6.13.2   It is the responsibility of staff in the child and adolescent service to establish as far as possible the grounds for any child protection concern which may exist, and to report this to the health board, having first informed the family.

6.13.3   While the health board holds overall responsibility for the child protection aspects of a case, it may be desirable for work to be done jointly between the two services in order to avoid fragmentation of services to families and to maximise the possibility of protecting any children involved. It is essential that information relevant to children's safety and protection is communicated between the two services at all stages of work.

6.14   Private Health Care

6.14.1   Professionals who see children and families on a private basis must follow child protection guidelines if they become concerned about a child's safety and welfare. It is the responsibility of the Child Care Manager/designate to ensure that, as far as possible, all private practitioners receive copies of procedures for communicating concerns to the health board.

6.15 Probation and Welfare Service

6.15.1 Probation officers may become involved in cases of child abuse as a result of their statutory responsibility for the supervision of offenders, including those convicted of offences against children. Probation officers also undertake the preparation of reports on people charged with criminal offences and the provision of welfare services for prisoners and those recently released from prison.

6.15.2 In the course of these duties, probation officers may encounter cases of child abuse or the risk of abuse. The Probation and Welfare Service should ensure that procedures are in place so that any potential, suspected or actual cases of child abuse are brought to the attention of the health board.

Responses of the
Health Board and
An Garda Síochána
to Child Abuse and
Children at Risk

part three

7 Support Services to Children and Families

7.1 Purpose

7.1.1 This chapter affirms the statutory responsibility of health boards to provide support services to the families of children who may be risk of abuse or neglect. It offers guidance on the delivery of services in a sensitive fashion which meets the individual needs of children and families, linking them with existing social supports in the community as well as providing a range of services through health boards and voluntary organisations.

7.1.2 Many of the children who come to the attention of the health board or other professionals are living in difficult and stressful environments. Their parents/carers may be experiencing relationship difficulties or domestic violence; there may be alcohol, drug or mental health problems; there may be a learning difficulty or a physical disability; or there may be some other source of stress. Children may consistently present with minor accidental injuries, have behavioural problems, miss school or appear unhappy. This does not necessarily mean that they are being abused but their needs for care and protection may not be adequately met in these circumstances and they may be at risk of future harm. Health boards are obliged under the Child Care Act 1991 to provide family support services to promote the welfare of children in such situations.

7.2 Family Support Services

7.2.1 Early intervention can help to prevent any worsening of current difficulties being experienced by a family and will assist the development and growth of protective factors. The delivery of family support also enables health boards to track cases where risks exist but where the situation does not warrant a child protection assessment.

7.2.2 Family support may be delivered formally through the direct services of statutory and voluntary organisations, and informally through the support of extended families, friends, neighbourhoods, communities, parishes and other local networks. Family support may or may not require the direct involvement of professionals, but where it is being provided to a family where children are considered to be at risk, it needs to be co-ordinated and monitored by the health board.

7.2.3 Each community care area should have a family support service plan, which should take account of the views of all relevant service providers and representatives of community organisations.

7.2.4 Family support services aim to achieve the following:

    (i) respond in a supportive manner to families where children's welfare is under threat;

    (ii) reduce risk to children by enhancing their family life;

    (iii) prevent avoidable entry of children into the care system;

    (iv) attempt to address current problems being experienced by children and families;

    (v) develop existing strengths of parents/carers and children who are under stress;

    (vi) enable families to develop strategies for coping with stress;

    (vii) provide an accessible, realistic and user-friendly service;

    (viii) connect families with supportive networks in the community;

    (ix) promote parental competence and confidence;

    (x) provide direct services to children;

    (xi) assist in the re-integration of children back into their families.

7.2.5 Effective family support services should have the following components:

    (i) a commitment to empowering families within their own communities;

    (ii) joint agreement between families and professionals about the type of support needed;

    (iii) a focus on the individual needs of children and parents/carers, considered separately and together;

    (iv) identification of a network of existing supports in the community such as extended family, neighbours, church groups, clubs and associations;

    (v) links with community based services such as playgroups, projects, schools and after-school programmes, local organisations, parenting programmes, adult education, family support services, child care services, health services;

    (vi) provision and ongoing resourcing of services as the need arises;

    (vii) availability of supports during a crisis or over a prolonged period;

    (viii) ongoing identification of needs within the community;

    (ix) ongoing evaluation of service provision.

7.3   Dimensions of Family Support

7.3.1 Family support services may be offered at three different levels. These are: services specifically directed at children; services to support the family; and services to enhance the friendship and support networks of the child and his/her family.

Services specifically directed at children

7.3.2 Services specifically directed at children aim to enhance the child's welfare by increasing his or her self confidence and social skills, developing special talents and abilities, helping the child to get over traumatic or damaging experiences, and carrying out primary and secondary preventive work. These services should be in line with the child's age and stage of development. Work could take place on a one-to-one basis in the child's home, in a community or group setting. If necessary, specialist consultants could be brought in to augment other support networks.

Services to Support Families

7.3.3 Services to support the family aim to enhance the skills of parents/carers by providing direct practical help, support and counselling. Work could be carried out at group or individual levels, either in community settings or family homes. Respite breaks for parents/carers and or children may be beneficial in certain situations. Services can include advocacy about housing, financial, health and other welfare needs

Services to Enhance Friendship and Support Networks

7.3.4 Services to enhance the friendship and support networks of the child and his/her family may involve working with extended family members and making links between the family and existing community resources. This may be done through workers in voluntary organisations or by drawing upon existing statutory services. Examples of community resources might be local community mothers who act as peer educators, parents'/carers' groups, pre-school programmes in early childhood, school-based and after-school programmes for older children, and Neighbourhood Youth Projects for adolescents.

7.4 Guidelines on the Delivery of Family Support Services

7.4.1 Parents/carers as well as children themselves may request a service directly from the health board, or they may be referred by another source. A request for services should be responded to in a supportive and non-threatening manner. Families should be encouraged to identify their own solutions as much as possible. The effective delivery of family support services will depend a number of factors including the following:

> (i) the availability of good quality services from a range of agencies and professionals;
>
> (ii) the quality of assessment and planning conducted jointly by professionals and family members;
>
> (iii) the level of agreement reached between professionals and family members;
>
> (iv) the availability of services for as long as is necessary.

7.5 Assessment of the Need For Family Support Services

7.5.1 The aim of assessment is to gain sufficient understanding of the needs and strengths of the child and his/her parents/carers so that appropriate services can be identified, offered and agreed. The assessment can take place with individuals but should also be conducted jointly with all family members. A family support meeting is a useful venue for drawing up a plan and for consolidating any informal undertakings made. This meeting would be attended by the family, any other members of neighbourhood/community networks, and any professionals involved in delivering a service or offering support. The family should be assisted to set the agenda for this meeting. Tasks, including the person(s) responsible for carrying them out, can be identified and an outline plan agreed and recorded. A family group conference model may also be a useful mechanism for drawing up a family support plan (see **Appendix Six**).

7.5.2 Assessment of a family's needs for support should take account of the following:

(i) perception of problems and concerns by each family member;

(ii) perception of problems and concerns by other persons such as reporters, professionals, extended family, concerned other persons;

(iii) the level of risk to children which is believed to exist;

(iv) solutions which are jointly informed by the family's perception of their needs and the expertise of those providing services;

(v) existing family strengths and protective factors;

(vi) acceptable informal supports already available;

(vii) acceptable informal supports potentially available;

(viii) formal supports available;

(ix) formal supports which need to be made available.

7.6   Family Support Plan

7.6.1 A family support plan should take the following factors into account:

(i) the level of agreement which either exists or is negotiable between the perceptions held by parents/carers and others such as family members, professionals, concerned other persons;

(ii) the part of the problem which needs the most urgent attention;

(iii) short and long term goals;

(iv) available and potential options;

(v) access to necessary resources;

(vi) specified persons, disciplines or agencies which need to be involved;

(vii) the length of time that family support services may be required bearing in mind that some families will need assistance only in times of crisis, others over a longer period;

(viii) allowing time for evaluation and review.

7.7 Family Support Agreement

7.7.1 While the emphasis in family support should be on partnership and support of community initiatives, there will be certain situations where contractual agreement between the family and service providers would be desirable. Any such agreement should specify the following:

(i) mutual expectations held by the family and the providers of services and supports;

(ii) shared understandings of the type of services and supports sought and provided;

(iii) responsibilities of the family;

(iv) responsibilities of the providers of services and supports;

(v) goals and targets to be achieved by a named date;

(vi) contingency plans.

7.7.2 Families are well positioned to identify and prioritise their needs although they may need support to do so and to judge whether the services offered are helpful.

Assessment and Management

8.1 Purpose

8.1.1 This chapter offers guidance on the steps to be taken by health board workers in responding to reported child protection concerns. It outlines the responsibility of the health board and describes the assessment process which should be followed in order to establish whether reasonable grounds for concern exist. The importance of considering existing strengths and protective factors in the child and family situation is also highlighted. The chapter also offers guidance on the effective use of child protection conferences, the basic components of a child protection plan and the aims and objectives of child protection reviews. While the emphasis throughout is primarily on responding to child protection concerns, children and their parents/carers need to be treated with fairness, respect and sensitivity at all times.

8.2 Responsibility of the Health Board

8.2.1 Health board staff are obliged to treat seriously all child protection concerns, whatever their source, and consider carefully and fairly the nature of the information reported. Whatever response is considered most appropriate, a balance needs to be struck between protecting the child and avoiding unnecessary and distressing intervention. The health board response must:

> (i) consider the protection and welfare of the child as a priority;
>
> (ii) avoid actions which cause the child or family undue distress;
>
> (iii) respect the rights of parents/carers and children to have their views heard and to be fully informed of any steps taken.

8.3 Confidentiality and Anonymity

8.3.1 All information regarding concern or assessment of child abuse should be shared on "a need to know" basis in the interests of the child.

8.3.2 No undertakings regarding secrecy can be given. Those working with a child and family should make this clear to all parties involved.

8.3.2 Concerns about child abuse which are reported anonymously should be followed up by the health board, depending on the content of the report made, and the nature of any other information about the child which may be held by the health board. However, reporters should be informed that anonymity might restrict the ability of professionals to access information or to intervene to protect a child. As much openness as possible should be encouraged. If the report has been made through a third party, the person mediating should be requested to facilitate contact between the original reporter and the health board.

8.4 Record Keeping

8.4.1 Record keeping is of critical importance in this area of work. Unless accurate records are maintained, the ability to adequately protect vulnerable children may be severely curtailed. It is essential that professionals keep contemporaneous records of **all** reported child protection concerns; this should include details of contacts, consultations and any actions taken.

8.4.2 Case notes are kept in order to:

(i) record details of referral, investigation and assessments of child care concerns;

(ii) record essential details concerning the child and his or her parents/carers

(iii) record the nature and level of services offered as well as those which are required;

(iv) establish a record which may be accessed by a number of professionals and agencies;

(v) record and review developments in a case;

(vi) provide a tool for use in the supervision of professional work;

(vii) establish a measure of accountability between practitioners and their line managers;

(viii) facilitate case transfers or the transfer of information between key professionals from different areas.

8.4.3 Each profession and organisation may have their own style of record-keeping which should detail their involvement in each case and record all contacts and significant events. Voluntary organisations that administer services through a number of individual units should aim to standardise recording procedures in cases of children at risk. All agencies dealing with children must have a policy of co-operating with the health board in sharing of their records. Standardised record systems should be adopted by hospitals in order to highlight repeated visits by children presenting with injuries (see Chapter Six on individual and corporate responsibility). The management of records held by the **health board social worker or other designated key worker** should be standardised in each health board area. Each file should contain the following in chronological order:

(i) a summary sheet containing family details, to be kept at the front of the file;

(ii) a record of all enquiries made about the case and the responses obtained;

(iii) a record of all contacts between the worker and the child and his or her parents/carers;

(iv) a record of all contacts between the worker and other professionals, including working arrangements and agreements;

(v) a summary, to be updated three monthly on recent events and their significance;

(vi) a report of all court proceedings, child protection conferences, reviews and any other meetings as well as any other relevant documentation in the worker's possession;

(vii) details of assessment procedures and outcomes;

(viii) a record of any decisions made;

(ix) a copy of any child protection plans;

(x) a copy of all correspondence about the case.

8.4.4 Records should be factual, accurate and legible and should be dated and signed after **each** entry. If an assessment or evaluation is made, an explanation for its basis must be offered.

8.4.5 Records should be accessible at all times during a key worker's absence. It is the responsibility of line managers to ensure that files are kept up to date and good recording practices are maintained.

8.4.6 Notwithstanding the requirement of all professionals involved in child protection cases to share relevant information, records are nevertheless confidential. They do not belong to individuals (except for independent practitioners) and are the property of the organisations that keep them. Under the **Freedom of Information Act, 1997** members of the public have a right of access to records held by any public body concerning them and a right to have official information about themselves amended where it is incorrect, incomplete or misleading. Members of the public also have a right to be given reasons for decisions made concerning themselves. Requests to see records are processed in the first instance through the public body which holds the records. In the event in the refusal of access, the decision may be appealed and the ultimate arbiter is the Information Commissioner.

8.5   Child Protection Assessment

8.5.1 The process involved in the assessment of reported concerns about child protection is outlined in Figure 8.1. It is important to note that this is a generic model of assessment and that, depending on the circumstances of individual cases, other models may be used. In addition, not all cases will follow this precise sequence; for example, in certain circumstances it may be necessary to move directly from Phase One to Phase Three.

Figure 8.1 Child Protection Assessment/Investigation Process

PHASE ONE	**ALLEGATION OF CHILD ABUSE** ↓ **REFERRAL TO HEALTH BOARD SOCIAL WORK DEPARTMENT** ↓ **SOCIAL WORKER CONSULTS RECORDS & MAKES INITIAL ENQUIRIES** (both internal and external enquiries) ↓ **SOCIAL WORKER CONSULTS WITH LINE MANAGER** (Team Leader or Senior Social Worker) Matters to be considered at this point include: • Co-ordination of information • Contact and discussion with child and parents/carers • Contact with person who first reported concern • Assessment of risk and protective factors* • Emergency action/reception into care • Medical examination • Referral to services, including support services for children and families • Immediate intervention • Further information gathering • No further action • Feedback to reporters

PHASE TWO	**NOTIFICATION TO CHILD CARE MANAGER** Options to be considered at this point include:

Notification to An Garda Síochána	Strategy Meeting	*Health Board Assessment*
• Garda investigation • Key interviews and review • Prepare file for Director of Public Prosecutions (DPP) • DPP reviews file • DPP decision due	Consult with: • Family • Team Leader/Senior Social Worker • Child Care Manager • Legal advisor • An Garda Síochána-Health Board Liaison Team Assess risks and protective factors: • medical input • legal input • psychosocial input	• Assessment by health board social worker or other professional • Placement on Child Protection Notification System • Referral to other specialist assessment teams • Ongoing contact with child and parents/carers • Continued liaison with relevant professionals • Emergency action/court reception into care • Record everything

PHASE THREE	**CHILDREN PROTECTION CONFERENCE** • Further evaluation of risk • Negotiation of a comprehensive inter-agency child protection plan between professionals and family • Allociation of tasks • Treatment intervention • Review of progress **CHILD PROTECTION REVIEW**

* If it appears that a Garda investigation may be likely, consultation should be held with An Garda Síochna at this stage.

8.6 Initial Response to a Reported Child Protection Concern

8.6.1 Reported concerns about child protection are normally followed up by a **health board social worker.** If internal records indicate that a case is already open and known to a health board or other agency, the key professionals involved should be contacted immediately.

8.6.2 All concerns about child protection which are reported to a health board must be taken seriously and recorded.

PHASE ONE: PRELIMINARY ENQUIRIES

8.7 Assessment Procedures

8.7.1 Professional staff who assess reported concerns about child protection will need to consider systematically the following:

(i) the nature and degree of any child abuse indicated in the report;

(ii) the potential and current impact of suspected abuse on each child in the family;

(iii) the need to take immediate protective action;

(iv) the necessity to confer with professionals and agencies who may be involved already with the child and family;

(v) the need to formally notify the Child Care Manager/designate of the report.

8.7.2 All health board records must be checked at the earliest opportunity, in order to establish whether a child or family are known to the child protection services and the nature of any information available. It may be necessary to contact the relevant public health nurse, area medical officer, social worker, child care worker or other health board colleague for information or for clarification of existing information.

8.7.3 Non-health board agencies or professionals may have relevant information to contribute to the assessment of a concern about child protection. These may include general practitioners, teachers, counsellors and other services with which the child and/or parents/carers have had contact. Information should normally only be sought from professionals working outside the health board when the parents/carers concerned have been informed that such an enquiry is taking place. However, in circumstances where the perceived risk to the child is such that it is not deemed desirable to contact parents/carers in the first instance, a health board professional could justifiably request non-health board professionals to release whatever information might enable clarification of the initial reported concern about child abuse.

8.7.4 If, on the basis of the reported concern, and/or any existing information, there is reason to believe that a child has been harmed or is at risk of further harm, or that their safety and welfare are at risk, the concern must be followed up immediately and any necessary interventions made. The available information should be reviewed with senior management and formally recorded in order to establish an appropriate level of response.

8.8 Provision of Alternative Services

8.8.1 In some situations, initial reports or enquiries may indicate that the concern does not warrant notification to the Child Care Manager/designate even though the child's welfare needs are not being adequately met. In such situations, the provision of **support services** could prevent further deterioration in the situation and reduce any actual or potential risk (see Chapter Seven on Support Services to Children and Families).

8.9 Emergency Action to Protect A Child

8.9.1 If a report made to the health board indicates the presence of immediate and serious risk, urgent action must be taken to protect any children in that situation who may be in danger. This may mean securing the co-operation of a protective carer, family member, or other responsible adult in the child's home whose capacity to protect the child can be defined and agreed.

8.9.2 If it is not possible to make arrangements to have the child or children protected at home, they may need to be removed to an appropriate location, preferably with the consent of the parents/carers, but if necessary using legal measures under the Child Care Act, 1991. If emergency action has not already been agreed, consultation must take place between the practitioners involved and their line managers. Interventions involving the separation of children from their parents/carers can only be carried out by properly authorised officers with delegated powers from the Chief Executive Officer of the health board. Legal advice must be sought at an early stage if court action is planned.

8.9.3 It must be borne in mind that the removal of children from their parents/carers or their homes can be very stressful and requires sensitive handling. The likely effects of separation must be balanced against the danger of leaving the child at home; all means of protecting the child at home must be considered first.

8.9.4 If it is considered necessary to remove a child from his/her carers, then the following must be considered:

(i) All possible efforts should be made to place the child in a situation which is familiar, preferably with family or friends [see Child Care (Placement of Children with Relatives) Regulations, 1995 which have been published by the Department of Health and Children].

(ii) As far as possible, the timing of the move should be sensitively handled.

(iii) The child's parents/carers should be informed of the action which is proposed, unless doing so would endanger the child or jeopardise the placement process.

(iv) The child should be informed of the proposed action if (s)he has not been involved in the decision.

(v) The child's parents/carers should be informed of the child's location unless otherwise directed by the court.

(vi) The child's parents/carers should be advised and assisted about obtaining legal advice.

8.9.5 In the majority of cases, the perceived harm or risk does not warrant such emergency action and the concern should be followed up in a **planned, co-ordinated manner**. This involves communicating with all professionals involved with the child and enlisting their assistance if appropriate.

8.10 Routine Steps to be Undertaken by Health Board Staff and Other Involved Professionals when Making Enquiries about Children's Care and Protection

8.10.1 All child protection concerns reported to the health board must be followed up as soon as possible. It is normally the role of the health board social worker to carry out this task. However this role may be allocated by the social work manager to another professional or agency closely involved with the family. Alternatively, the work may be carried out jointly between the health board and another agency. In these circumstances, the expectations held by the health board of any non-health board professionals or agency must be made clear. **Any professional involved in following up child protection concerns must report the outcome of their enquiries without delay to the health board social worker manager.**

8.10.2 A number of key tasks are involved in making a child protection enquiry. These include the following:

(i) establishing with the child and his/her parents/carers whether grounds for concern exist;

(ii) if necessary, arranging for a medical examination, assessment for child sexual abuse and medical treatment (see paragraph 8.13 also);

(iii) communicating with any professionals involved with child and family and eliciting their views on the report of abuse;

(iv) identifying the nature and severity of any risks;

(v) identifying any strengths and protective factors which appear to lessen the risk such as protective care, support of extended family member or friend, existing family support service;

(vi) deciding on initial protective action pending, or prior to, further action such as investigation, child protection conference discussion or comprehensive assessment.

8.10.3 The assessment of a child protection concern can often be complicated by factors outside the control of the professionals involved and does not always resemble the ordered process described in these National Guidelines. The safety and welfare of a child must remain a priority throughout and the remainder of the tasks covered in the most efficient and expeditious manner possible. Any difficulties in accessing information must be recorded and brought to the attention of social work manager/child care manager.

8.11 Interviewing Parents/Carers

8.11.1 When a concern about a child's care or protection is reported to the health board, the child's parents/carers should be contacted by health board social worker or other professional who has agreed to carry out this task. It must be borne in mind that the experience of being reported to the health board about the care and protection of one's children can be both traumatic and intimidating for parents/carers; sensitivity must be used in conducting the interviews. The quality of any relationship which may later exist between the family and professionals will be influenced by the manner in which this initial meeting is handled.

8.11.2 If An Garda Síochána have already been notified and are likely to be carrying out a joint investigation, it is essential that the activities of the two organisations are agreed and co-ordinated (see Chapter Nine on An Garda Síochána-Health Board Protocol) .

8.11.3 All professionals, whether health board or not, should observe the following procedures when interviewing parents/carers:

> (i) inform parents/carers in an open and honest way of existing concerns and reports about their child/children;
>
> (ii) explain how information about the case has been, and will be, obtained;
>
> (iii) identify the professionals who are, or who have been, contacted so far;
>
> (iv) invite the parents/carers to give an explanation of their view of the concern;
>
> (v) show a willingness to consider different interpretations of the concern;
>
> (vi) ensure that the parents/carers are fully aware of the way that information is going to be assessed and evaluated and what expectations are held of them about the way they care for and protect their children;
>
> (vii) if relevant, explain the legal context in which the concern is being investigated;
>
> (viii) if the concern arose from an incident perpetrated by one of a child's parents/carers, the worker should try to gain the support and co-operation of the other parent/carer to facilitate on-going protection of the child.

Conflict between Parents and Children

8.11.4 Where the interests of the parents and the child appear to conflict, the child's interests must be considered paramount. It may be necessary to provide a separate worker for each of the parents/carers if, for example, one parent/carer is the alleged abuser.

8.12   Interviewing a Child

8.12.1   In the course of child protection work, different types of interviews may be carried out with children. The interview referred to in this section concerns the meeting which takes place between a health board worker and a child in the initial stages of a child protection enquiry. In most instances, depending on the nature of the concern, the child should be seen by the professional conducting the enquiry and spoken to personally, in a manner appropriate to his or her age and stage of development. **The child should not usually be interviewed in detail about sexual or serious physical abuse. This may be more appropriately done at a later stage by specialist personnel or An Garda Síochána, or both.**

8.12.2   The interview should take place in a location which is comfortable for the child and, if the child desires it, in the presence of a support person such as a protective parent/carer, another professional or an adult friend. If the child has a learning disability or sensory impairment, it may be necessary to employ expert assistance to facilitate communication. **It is important that the child is not interviewed in the company of any person who may have a vested interest in their version of events or who might influence what the child may say.**

8.12.3   Interviews with children should normally be carried out with their parents'/carers' permission and the child must be able to give his or her own consent.

8.12.4   In some circumstances, children may present themselves to a health board social worker without either the knowledge or presence of their parents/carers. Depending on the perceived maturity of the child, the social worker should give them the opportunity to discuss whatever concerns have prompted them to make contact. In some areas, the child is interviewed jointly by An Garda Síochána and other professionals. This avoids the need for repeated interviews. Where this is the policy, local protocols should be observed.

8.12.5   No avoidable action should be taken which will cause a child to feel intimidated or distressed. The worker must use language which the child can understand and explain who they are and why they are there. It is essential to conduct the interview at the child's pace and communicate with him or her in a warm and responsive manner.

8.12.6   The reasons for interviewing the child include the following:

  (i)   to get a picture of the child's physical and emotional state;

  (ii) to establish whether the child needs urgent medical attention;

  (iii) to hear the child's version of the circumstances leading to the concern;

  (iv) to get a picture of the child's relationship with his or her parents/carers;

  (v)   to support the child to participate in decisions affecting him or her according to his or her age and maturity;

  (vi) to find out who the child trusts;

  (vii) to inform the child of any further steps to be taken in the enquiry.

8.12.7 It is the responsibility of the health board to ensure that staff carrying out child protection enquiries have sufficient training and experience in interviewing children. If the child is not present and the parents/carers are not willing to co-operate in allowing him or her to be seen, the matter should be brought to the attention of the worker's line manager, and a decision made regarding any further action.

8.13 Medical/Specialist Examinations

8.13.1 If there is reason to believe that a medical examination will indicate more clearly whether or not a child has been physically abused, or seriously deprived or neglected, or if a child appears to require medical treatment, then appropriate arrangements should be made immediately. Wherever possible, a doctor whom the child knows, and who is experienced in child abuse work should carry out an examination.

8.13.2 If there is reason to believe that a specialist assessment will indicate more clearly whether a child has been sexually abused, a referral should be made to the appropriate service. If any doubt exists as to whether referral to a specialist unit is required, the child sexual abuse assessment service for the area should be consulted for an opinion. A physical examination for sexual abuse should only be carried out by a doctor with appropriate training and experience.

8.13.3 In all cases where medical examinations or assessments for child sexual abuse are carried out, permission must be gained from the child's parents/carers. Parents/carers should be given the opportunity to attend. If permission is refused, the parents/carers should be advised of the health board's option to apply for an Emergency Care Order. Such action should be considered if co-operation is still withheld.

8.13.4 The medical or specialist practitioner who carries out the examination or assessment must give a written report of the findings, and must be made aware that he or she may be required to give evidence in court.

8.14 Feedback to Reporters

In all cases, persons who refer or discuss their concerns about the care and protection of children with health board staff should be informed of the likely steps to be taken by the professionals involved. Wherever appropriate and within the normal limits of confidentiality, health board staff have a responsibility to inform reporters and any other involved professionals about the outcomes of any enquiry or investigation into that reported concern.

PHASE TWO: NOTIFICATION TO CHILD CARE MANAGER/DESIGNATE

8.15 Child Protection Notification System

8.15.1 The Child Protection Notification System is a health board record of every child about whom, following a preliminary assessment, there is a child protection concern. A child's name is placed on the Child Protection Notification System by the Child Care Manager/designate following completion of a preliminary assessment (see **Appendix Seven**). Notifications to the Child Care Manager/designate must be on the Standard Notification Form (see **Appendix Eight**)

8.15.2 The Child Care Manager/designate has responsibility for ensuring that the following takes place:

> (i) a review meeting of all reports notified;
>
> (ii) the review meeting is held as soon as possible after the receipt of a notification;
>
> (iii) at six monthly intervals each report will be reviewed until a final outcome of the assessment is known and an agreed intervention has been put in place.

8.16 Strategy Meeting

8.16.1 At the outset of a child protection enquiry, when it appears that a child is at serious risk and may need immediate protection, it is vital to share all available and relevant information between the professionals most closely involved. At any point during a child protection enquiry it may be considered appropriate to convene a strategy meeting or discussion with all relevant professionals. This meeting can involve any, or all, of the professionals involved at either management or case assessment level, depending on the circumstances. It is particularly important to consider this process following preliminary enquiries and the submission of a Child Protection Notification Form to the Child Care Manager/designate (see **Appendix Eight**). It is essential that the attendance of a Garda Síochána representative is secured at this meeting especially if formal notification procedures are, or have been, invoked.

8.16.2 It is the responsibility of the health board social work team leader or social work manager to arrange a strategy meeting. The objectives of a strategy meeting are to:

> (i) share available information;
>
> (ii) consider whether immediate action should be taken to protect the child and other children in the same situation;
>
> (iii) consider available legal options;
>
> (iv) plan early intervention;
>
> (v) identify possible sources of protection and support for the child;
>
> (vi) identify sources of further information to facilitate the enquiry and assessment;
>
> (vii) allocate responsibility for further enquiry;
>
> (viii) agree with An Garda Síochána how the remainder of the enquiry will be conducted.

8.17 Roles and Responsibilities of Professionals Involved in Assessing Reported Concerns about Child Protection

8.17.1 It is normally the role of social workers in each health board to carry out enquiries into child protection concerns which have been reported to it. However, other disciplines such as public health nurses or clinical psychologists may be allocated this task in certain cases where, for example, they have a close relationship with the families concerned. If a child protection concern has been notified to An Garda Síochána, they may conduct a parallel investigation, in co-ordination with the health board (see An Garda Síochána-Health Board Protocol in Chapter Nine).

8.17.2 It is important that any professional making enquiries into a reported concern about child protection has first considered the issue of parents'/carers' co-operation. This is especially true if the professional is making enquiries of agencies external to the health board. It is possible for professionals who work in the health board to consult with their colleagues and check internal records at a preliminary stage. However, the parents/carers must be informed if the professional wishes to make enquiries of external agencies except in exceptional circumstances as outlined in 8.7.3.

8.17.3 Professionals in voluntary agencies, schools, clinics, or other settings are in a good position to observe a child and his or her relationship with parents/carers. It may be appropriate for a professional from one of these organisations to pursue the enquiry jointly with, or on behalf of, the health board. This should be negotiated with the social work manager in the health board.

8.17.4 When suspicions of child abuse exist but cannot be ascertained, health board social workers may encourage other professionals who are in contact with the child to use any possible opportunity available to them to substantiate or eliminate concerns in a sensitive manner. For example a teacher may observe a child's behaviour, interactions with peers, school work, or informal conversations. A therapist, child care worker, or anyone working with a child might gently explore the reasons for particular actions or statements, or use a play situation to enable the child to express him or herself. Any strategies used in this manner should be agreed with the health board social worker.

8.17.5 Professionals who are contacted by the health board for information about a child must be informed in due course of the outcome of the enquiry, where relevant to their professional concerns.

8.18 Assessment

8.18.1 It is the responsibility of the health board social worker or other key worker assigned to the enquiry to collate all the information which is available and make an initial assessment of risk to the child and any other children in the same situation.

8.18.2   The initial assessment is likely to be based on limited information and is mainly concerned with the child's immediate safety. It should consider the following factors about the child and his or her parents/carers:

    (i) the child's physical and emotional state as well as his or her wishes regarding immediate intervention;

    (ii) the nature and severity of any current harm being experienced by the child, taking into account the child's age and vulnerability;

    (iii) the likely nature and severity of any potential future harm if the child remains in the care of his or her parents/carers;

    (iv) the presence or absence at home of the alleged perpetrator;

    (v) current stresses and problems being experienced by the family;

    (vi) the presence of positive factors in a child's environment, including a protective parent/carer (such as one of the child's two parents/carers who has not been implicated in the reported concern), a supportive relative, or neighbour who has the capacity to protect the child as well as any supports already in place;

    (vii) the needs of the child's family for immediate assistance and the provision of that assistance.

8.18.3   If grounds for concern still exist, further assessment involving a thorough consideration of all aspects of the child's situation should follow. This process may continue over a period of time, and may include a Child Protection Conference (see section 8.19 below). The process consists of the different stages of information gathering, analysis, assessment and decision making. The assessment is normally co-ordinated by a health board social worker but this responsibility may be assigned by the social work team leader/social worker manager to another professional who is appropriately experienced and has frequent contact with the child and his or her parents/carers. It may require the involvement of clinical psychologists, paediatricians, addiction services, psychiatric services and child sexual abuse assessment services.

8.18.4   The essential components of a full assessment are:

    (i) gathering information through interviews and child protection conference discussions and conclusions;

    (ii) co-ordinating and analysing information on the child and his or her key relationships, the child's parents/carers, the child's familial and social networks including school;

    (iii) considering any contextual factors such as mental health problems, addiction, disability or other difficulties which may impact on the child's safety and the ability of parents/carers to meet his or her needs;

    (iv) evaluating the level of risk and potential for positive intervention;

    (v) formulating a child protection plan and recommending protective interventions.

8.18.5 In addition to identifying risk factors, it is important to note the positive aspects and strengths of each situation, including the quality and efficacy of services already in place. Assessment should be based on the gravity of risks balanced against their manageability relative to the age and stage of development of the child. At all times, the welfare of the child must be the first priority.

8.18.6 If it is decided that further child protection enquiry or assessment is unnecessary, the need for support services to the child and family should be considered (see Chapter Seven on Child and Family Supports and Services).

8.18.7 All professionals and agencies involved must keep a contemporaneous record of all steps involved in enquiries and assessments. Case files should record all decisions, including a decision not to proceed with an enquiry, and specify the evidence or reasons upon which these are based. Records must always be accessible in the absence of a worker.

8.18.8 Records should always document the outcome of an investigation and assessment of a child protection concern, under one of the following headings:

> (i) confirmed abuse;
>
> (ii) assessment ongoing;
>
> (iii) inconclusive outcome;
>
> (iv) confirmed non-abuse/unfounded.

Outcomes must be notified in writing, following the local protocol, to the Child Care Manager/designate.

PHASE THREE: CASE MANAGEMENT

8.19 The Child Protection Conference

8.19.1 A child protection conference is an inter-agency and inter-professional meeting which is convened by the Child Care Manager/designate. It normally takes place when initial enquiries and, if relevant, emergency action have taken place. It may take place during the early stages of enquiry, or at any time when concerns arise about a child's care and protection. The child's parents/carers and the child should be included where appropriate. In cases where there is a language barrier, a disability, or sensory impairment, those with particular expertise (eg. interpreters) could also be included where necessary.

8.19.2 It is appropriate to hold a child protection conference when decisions of a serious nature are being considered which require the input of a number of professionals from different disciplines and agencies.

8.19.3 The main tasks of a child protection conference are:

(i) to facilitate the sharing and evaluation of information between professionals and carers;

(ii) to outline a child protection plan to be completed following comprehensive assessment;

(iii) to identify tasks to be carried out by different professionals.

8.19.4 Not all child protection situations warrant the convening of a child protection conference and it should not be used as a substitute for normal consultation or supervision, inadequate inter-professional or inter-agency arrangements or relationships, or convened for any other reason not directly related to the requirements of the particular case. **A decision for or against the holding of a child protection conference to discuss a child protection concern should be clearly documented.**

8.19.5 A child protection conference brings together the following categories of people:

(i) personnel who have specific responsibility in child protection;

(ii) practitioners from various disciplines and organisations who are currently involved with the child and the parents/carers;

(iii) professionals who may offer specialist or expert advice;

(iv) staff who may in the future be required to offer services;

(v) the child's parents/carers and, where appropriate, the child.

8.19.6 Only professionals whose involvement is central to the case should be invited to a child protection conference since meetings which are too large inhibit discussion and may intimidate families. Persons who have only peripheral involvement in a case may have their views represented by submitting written reports to be considered by the chairperson. Professionals whose presence is necessary to enable the child protection conference to fulfil its aims should always endeavour to attend. In cases of unavoidable absence, their views should be represented in writing to the Child Care Manager/designate outlining their factually-based opinions regarding the current concerns, past and present involvement, and information about the family.

8.19.7 Each area should establish a protocol for the conduct of child protection conferences which takes into account any special local arrangements. The purpose of the protocol is to promote good practices and make the best possible use of the professional and family time involved. It is the responsibility of the Child Care Manager/designate and managers of voluntary agencies and other organisations who are likely to participate in child protection conferences, to ensure that their staff are familiar with the local protocol. A child protection conference protocol is outlined in **Appendix Six**. The potential of teleconferencing and other technologies should be borne in mind when organising child protection conferences.

8.20 Appointment of a Key Worker

8.20.1 When a recommendation is made to offer services to a child and his or her parents/carers, the case must be allocated to a key worker if this has not already happened. All practitioners must receive regular supervision from an appropriate line manager.

8.21 The Child Protection Plan

8.21.1 The child protection plan is an inter-agency plan based on the outcome of assessment, together with the recommendations of the child protection conference, if one has been held. It is normally drawn up by the health board social worker in consultation with all parties involved, including the child and his or her parents/carers. It outlines the action which professionals and agencies directly involved with the family need to take in order to ensure the child's continued protection and well-being. The basic components of a child protection plan are:

(i) completion of comprehensive assessment;

(ii) identification of current and potential sources of risk to a child;

(iii) identification of strategies to protect the child and reduce the risks over a specified period;

(iv) identification of protective aspects of the child's situation, which may need to be strengthened and developed;

(v) identification of short-term and long-term goals to be achieved;

(vi) consultation and negotiation with the child and his or her parents/carers regarding the content and feasibility of the plan;

(vii) consideration of the position of the abuser and need for treatment;

(viii) clear allocation of specific roles and responsibilities to all professionals and agencies directly involved in implementing the plan;

(ix) clear allocation of the roles and responsibilities to the child's parents/carers and other relevant family members;

(x) identification of resources necessary to carry out the plan, including family support and treatment services where required;

(xi) identification of a key worker who will continue to co-ordinate the work of various personnel involved in carrying out the plan and who will be responsible for ensuring communication of information between all the parties involved.

8.21.2 When a child protection plan has been agreed, it is the responsibility of all identified professionals and agencies to implement those parts of the plan which relate to them and to communicate with the key worker. In order to ensure that the plan is implemented, the following conditions must be observed:

(i) each professional must be given a written copy of the plan;

(ii) a written copy of the plan should be given to the child, depending on his or her age and stage of development, and to his or her parents/carers;

(iii) the key worker must ensure that the child and family understand the nature and objectives of the plan;

(iv) the specific expectations of all parties about the plan and its implementation must be clarified;

(v) in addition to consultation about the plan, the child and his or her parents/carers should be given the names of all personnel involved in implementing the plan together with their specific roles;

(vi) any changes of personnel should be immediately notified to the child and his or her parents/carers.

8.21.3 The successful implementation of a child protection plan will depend on four functions: inter-agency and inter-professional co-operation; ongoing consultation with the child and his or her parents/carers; ongoing assessment; supervision and support.

8.21.4 **Inter-agency and inter-professional co-operation:** Co-operation between disciplines and agencies is as crucial to the longer term management of a case as it is at the outset. Commitment and flexibility in relation to carrying out the work specified in the child protection plan, together with willingness to exchange information promptly will be required from all professionals who are involved with the child.

8.21.5 **Ongoing consultation with the child and his or her parents/carers:** The views of the child and family must be sought on an ongoing basis and considered in relation to modifying the child protection plan.

8.21.6 **Ongoing assessment:** The protection and welfare of the child should be assessed on a continual basis to take account of changes in circumstances.

8.21.7 **Supervision and support:** All front line practitioners working with children and families in the cases should have consistent and regular support and supervision.

8.22 Case Transfer

8.22.1 Guidance on the steps to be taken when a child and his or her parents/carers move to another jurisdiction is contained in Chapter Nine (paragraph 9.16) which deals with An Garda Síochána-Health Board Protocol and in **Appendix Nine**.

8.22.2 Where children are considered to be at risk, and move from one area to another, the Child Care Manager/designate in the new area must be notified immediately and plans should be made to transfer responsibility for the case. The transfer should be fully completed within three months of the change of residence, and take place in a formal setting such as a child protection conference or review meeting. There must be a full exchange of all records on the case, whether held by the health board or by other organisations, including a summary report on the situation to date. The child and parents/carers should be involved in the transfer meeting and must be informed in writing of the names of all professionals involved in the new area.

8.23 Closure or Cessation of Involvement by Professionals

8.23.1 Professionals may withdraw from involvement with cases for various reasons or the social work manager may decide to terminate the health board social work involvement in a case on the basis that the concern no longer exists or is being satisfactorily addressed. Cases must only be closed when children are no longer considered at risk. When a case is closed, all professionals involved and the child and family must be informed. Ideally, closure would ensue following a review, but if not, the Child Care Manager/designate must endorse the decision.

8.24 Child Protection Reviews

8.24.1 Child protection reviews are held at six monthly intervals in all cases where the following conditions are met:

> (i) the child has been notified to the Child Care Manager/designate;
>
> (ii) the child is residing with his or her parents/carers
>
> (iii) the child is still considered to be at risk.

8.24.2 It is the responsibility of the Child Care Manager/designate to arrange reviews. Reviews should be attended by the core group of professionals involved with the case and each should submit a written report in advance to the chairperson. The child's parents/carers should attend unless a specific reason for their exclusion is identified. Children may be involved depending on their age and level of understanding.

8.24.3 The child protection review has a number of purposes, including the following:

> (i) to build up a picture of the child's current situation;
>
> (ii) to co-ordinate the views of professionals;
>
> (iii) to consider the views of the child and parents/carers;
>
> (iv) to review the progress of any legal action or prosecution if relevant;
>
> (v) to review and amend the child protection plan;
>
> (vi) to assess the availability of resources needed to carry out the child protection plan;

The child protection review should be minuted as soon as possible and copies of the proceedings should be circulated to all professionals involved as well as the child and parents/carers. If the child and parents/carers have not attended the review, an explanation should be given to them by the key worker of its contents, conclusions and implications.

8.25 Case Management Reviews

8.25.1 A case management review is a multi-agency review of the response, manner and quality of services provided to children and families. It is a systems check, the purpose of which is to learn lessons from the handling of specific cases so that deficits in the system can be addressed. Health boards will generally be responsible for instigating a case management review as part of their overall role in monitoring standards of service provision and delivery.

8.25.2 A case management review must be carried out in the following circumstances:

(i)   when the case of suspected or confirmed abuse involves the death of a child;

(ii) when the case of suspected or confirmed abuse involves the serious injury of a child;

(iii) when a child protection issue arises which is likely to be of significant public concern.

8.25.3 Case management reviews have a number of specific objectives including:

(i)   to establish facts;

(ii) to assess decision-making and interventions made in the case;

(iii) to check whether procedures have been followed;

(iv) to check whether services provided were adequate and appropriate;

(v)   to make recommendations in light of the findings.

9 An Garda Síochána-Health Board Protocol

9.1 Introduction

9.1.1 The health board and An Garda Síochána are the key agencies empowered by law to carry out the assessment and investigation of suspected child abuse. Each agency manages the responsibility within their brief and their joint efforts ensure that the protection of vulnerable children receives priority attention. The separate and complementary roles require careful understanding if the shared objectives of child protection are to be realised. An Garda Síochána have the additional responsibility of bringing abusers to justice.

9.2 Designated Personnel

9.2.1 It is essential that the health board and An Garda Síochána designate personnel at investigation and management levels who will remain involved with the case until the investigation is completed.

9.2.2 It is proposed that a social work Team Leader from the health board and designated district-based Inspector/Sergeant from within An Garda Síochána would constitute a **liaison management team,** whose functions comprise the following:

> (i) to consider notifications;
>
> (ii) to assign personnel and supervise investigation;
>
> (iii) to review progress in the case.

9.3 Tracking Systems

9.3.1 It is important for both the health board and An Garda Síochána to chart the progress of an investigation into a notified suspicion of child abuse. It is proposed that a standardised Joint Action Sheet be used to assist managers and other personnel in this task (see **Form 9.3** at the end of this chapter). The adoption of this procedure should ensure accountability in all cases.

9.4 Cases to be Notified by Health Boards to An Garda Síochána

9.4.1 Where a health board suspects that a child has been **physically or sexually abused or wilfully neglected,** An Garda Síochána must be formally notified in accordance with the procedure set out below. The process of establishing whether grounds exist for suspecting such abuse may involve consulting relevant professional personnel within the health board and, where appropriate, in outside agencies. Where appropriate, advice and guidance on the criminal law should be sought from An Garda Síochána. However, a health board

must not await confirmation of such abuse, whether from a child abuse assessment unit or otherwise, before notifying An Garda Síochána.

9.4.2   In all cases, the health board must inform the person reporting a suspicion of child abuse that their information will be shared with An Garda Síochána.

9.4.3   Health boards are not expected to routinely notify suspected cases of **emotional abuse or unintentional neglect** to An Garda Síochána since the circumstances of such cases may not involve law enforcement issues. However, in case of doubt, An Garda Síochána should be consulted.

9.4.4   On occasion, the health board may become aware of "indirect" abuse to children. this could occur if children have been photographed, videotaped or filmed without their knowledge, for pornographic purposes. This information should be conveyed to An Garda Síochána .

9.4.5   The procedure for notifying An Garda Síochána of a suspected case of physical or sexual abuse or wilful neglect of a child is as follows:

> (i) The Child Care Manager/designate sends the Standard Notification Form to the local Garda Superintendent (see **Form 9.1** at the end of this chapter). A copy is retained in the file on each child. Where more than one child is involved, a separate Standard Notification Form should be sent in respect of each child.
>
> (ii) On receipt of the Standard Notification Form, the Garda Superintendent arranges to have a designated Garda assigned to the case and immediately informs the Child Care Manager/designate of the Garda's name and station.
>
> (iii) The designated Garda makes direct contact without delay with the social worker (or other designated person) dealing with the case to obtain details of the case.
>
> (iv) When contact is established both the designated Garda and the social worker commence completion of the Joint Action Sheet (see **Form 9.3** at the end of this chapter).
>
> (v) At the same time, the Garda Superintendent will assign a designated Inspector/Sergeant to manage the investigation, monitor its progress and consult with the appointed health board manager of the case.
>
> (vi) Where contact cannot be established between the designated Garda and the social worker, the matter will revert immediately to the Social Work Team Leader of the case and the designated Garda Inspector/Sergeant for resolution.

9.5   Informal Consultation

9.5.1   In cases where the health board is aware of concerns about a child but is unable to establish sufficient grounds for formal notification, they should consult with An Garda Síochána on an informal basis. Such contact is to be actively encouraged in order to protect the welfare of the child concerned.

9.6   Emergency Intervention

9.6.1   In circumstances where a child's immediate safety is deemed to be at risk, the health board is obliged take immediate protective action. It is essential to inform An Garda Síochána as soon as possible of any actions taken or planned. A Standard Notification Form should be forwarded as soon as circumstances permit (see **Form 9.1 and Form 9.2** at the end of this chapter).

9.7   Cases to be Notified by An Garda Síochána to the Health Board

9.7.1   Where An Garda Síochána suspect that a child has been the victim of **emotional, physical or sexual abuse or neglect** (whether wilful or unintentional), the health board must be formally notified. It is not necessary for An Garda Síochána to have sufficient evidence to support a criminal prosecution before notifying the health board.

9.7.2   It is not intended that An Garda Síochána should notify the health board of cases of physical or sexual assaults against children which involve issues of law enforcement only; for example, cases involving the assault of a child by a stranger. An Garda Síochána should notify the health board of cases only if they give rise to child protection issues such as when the suspected abuser has ongoing contact with other children. In cases involving law enforcement only, An Garda Síochána should contact the health board where there is need for appropriate counselling and other support services for the victims of assaults.

9.7.3   An Garda Síochána may be involved in investigating a case of child abuse, or a retrospective disclosure of abuse, where the health board are not involved. Where appropriate, they should seek the advice of the health board regarding counselling and other support services for victims.

9.7.4   The procedure for notifying the health board of a suspected case of emotional, physical or sexual abuse or neglect of a child is as follows:

> (i) The Garda Superintendent sends the Standard Notification Form to the Child Care Manager/designate (see **Form 9.2** at the end of this chapter). A copy is held by the designated Garda dealing with the case and by the designated Garda Inspector/Sergeant. Where more than one child is involved, a separate Standard Notification Form should be sent in respect of each child.

(ii) On receipt of the notification form, the Child Care Manager/designate arranges to have a social worker (or other designated person) assigned to the case and immediately notifies the Garda Superintendent of the name and location of the designated social worker.

(iii) The social worker assigned to the case makes direct contact without delay with the designated Garda in charge of the case to obtain details of the case.

(iv) When contact is established, both the designated Garda and the social worker commence completion of the Joint Action Sheet (see **Form 9.3** at the end of this chapter).

(v) At the same time, the Child Care Manager will assign a designated social work Team Leader to manage the investigation, monitor its progress and consult with the appointed health board manager of the case.

(vi) Where contact cannot be established by the designated Garda or social workers, the matter will immediately revert to the Social Work Team Leader and the designated Garda Inspector/Sergeant for resolution.

9.7.5   The **liaison management team**, comprising the health board's social work Team Leader and the Garda Inspector/Sergeant, will be responsible for ensuring that inter-agency liaison occurs and that each Standard Notification Form is appropriately processed. Within An Garda Síochána, the notification process requires that the Standard Notification Form must be received by the investigating Garda, the designated Garda Inspector/Sergeant and the Garda Superintendent. Within the health board, the notification process requires that the Standard Notification Form must be received by the designated social worker, the designated social work Team Leader and the Child Care Manager/designate.

9.7.6   Figure 9.1 summarises An Garda Síochána-Health Board Notification Process.

Figure 9.1 An Garda Síochána-Health Board Notification Process

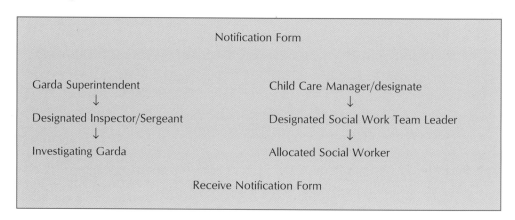

9.8   Informal Consultation

9.8.1   In cases where An Garda Síochána is aware of concerns about a child but is unable to establish sufficient grounds for formal notification to the health board, they should consult with the health board on an informal basis. Such contact is to be actively encouraged in order to protect the welfare of the child concerned.

9.9 Emergency Intervention

9.9.1 There may be occasions when An Garda Síochána has to take immediate action to protect a child without first notifying the health board. It is essential to inform the health board as soon as possible of any actions taken. A Standard Notification Form should be forwarded as soon as circumstances permit.

9.10 Investigation of Cases

9.10.1 It is essential that enquiries by the health board and An Garda Síochána should be co-ordinated to ensure that:

(i) the welfare of the child is protected;

(ii) everything possible is done to assist the criminal investigation and protect the available evidence;

(iii) there is a free flow of relevant information between agencies;

(iv) decisions and actions follow consultation within and between agencies.

9.11 Matters to be Considered During the Investigation and Management of Suspected Child Abuse Cases

9.11.1 **Allocation of Responsibility:** In cases where a specialist assessment of child sexual abuse is under-way, the early interviewing of the child by An Garda Síochána should be facilitated to ensure that statements may be obtained in a manner least likely to cause stress to the child. Some areas operate joint interviewing between An Garda Síochána and health board social workers, following local protocols. It is important to note that the person who initially reported the allegation of child sexual abuse or to whom the allegation was made may be a vital witness and should be interviewed by An Garda Síochána at an early stage.

9.11.2 **Record-Keeping:** The health board and An Garda Síochána should keep a written record of decisions taken in relation to the case. This record should be accessible in the absence of the specific personnel allocated to the case. It is recommended that all contacts between the health board and An Garda Síochána should be recorded. A decision which is made by either the health board or An Garda Síochána not to proceed must be recorded in detail.

9.11.3 **Child Protection Plan:** A child protection plan should be agreed by all persons involved. Plans will be reviewed on an ongoing basis (see Chapter Eight).

9.11.4 **Child Protection Conferences:** It is essential that the member of An Garda Síochána who is involved in the investigation of a case attend any strategy meetings or child protection conferences held. The invitation to attend should be sent in the first instance to the Garda Superintendent in order to facilitate the attendance of the designated Garda.

9.11.5 **Parental Involvement:** Every possible effort should be made to keep the child's parents/carers informed of developments in a case, except where this might place the child at further risk or impede the criminal investigation. It is common practice to invite parents/carers to attend child protection conferences. If this conflicts with the investigative process, the matter should be resolved between the relevant case managers, namely the social work Team Leader and the designated Inspector/Sergeant.

9.11.6 **Investigation of Organised Abuse:** The investigation of organised abuse requires particularly sensitive co-operation between health boards and An Garda Síochána. It may involve surveillance work and a higher degree of secrecy than would normally be expected in child protection work. It may be undesirable to share information fully with families in the early stages of investigation since breaches of confidentiality may seriously impede detection.

9.12   Confidentiality

9.12.1 It is essential that all information exchanged between the health board and An Garda Síochána is treated with the utmost confidentiality in order to safeguard the privacy of the children and families concerned and to avoid prejudicing any subsequent legal proceedings.

9.12.2 Regard must be had to The Freedom of Information Act, 1997 when considering a request for confidentiality. At present, the act applies to health boards but not to An Garda Síochána. In particular, cognisance should be taken of Section 23 (Law Enforcement and Public Safety) of The Freedom of Information Act, 1997 when considering concerns about the confidentiality of information. Health board records containing references to communications with An Garda Síochána will be considered "Third Party" records and, as such, will be referred to the Garda Commissioner when any request for information release under The Freedom of Information Act is being considered.

9.13   Ongoing Liaison

9.13.1 The health board social worker and the designated Garda should stay in regular contact and inform each other of developments in the case as they take place. The link between both agencies should be maintained until the criminal investigation and the prosecution (where applicable) is completed or until the child protection concerns are finalised.

9.13.2 Certain aspects of the investigation ought to be considered by both agencies, including the following:

> (i) impact of a prosecution on the victim;
>
> (ii) impact of the alleged abuse on the child;
>
> (iii) support for child and adult witnesses;
>
> (iv) victim support services.

9.14 Strategy Meeting

9.14.1 In addition to the initial strategy meeting, at any point during a child protection enquiry it may be appropriate to convene a strategy meeting or discussion with all relevant professionals. At the outset of a child protection enquiry, when it appears that a child is at serious risk and may need immediate protection, it is vital to share all available and relevant information between the professionals most closely involved. This meeting can involve all or any of the professionals involved at either management or case investigation level, depending on the circumstances. This process is also particularly important to consider following preliminary enquiries and the submission of a Standard Notification Form to the Child Care Manager/designate. It is essential that the attendance of An Garda Síochána representative is secured at this meeting especially if formal notification procedures are/have been invoked.

9.14.2 It is the responsibility of the health board social work team leader or social work manager to arrange a strategy meeting.

9.14.3 Strategy meetings have a number of objectives including:

(i) to share available information;

(ii) to consider whether immediate action should be taken to protect the child and other children in the family;

(iii) consider available legal options;

(iv) plan early intervention;

(v) identify possible sources of protection and support for the child;

(vi) identify sources of further information to facilitate the enquiry and assessment;

(vii) allocate responsibility for further enquiry;

(viii) agree with An Garda Síochána how the remainder of the enquiry will be conducted.

9.15 Special Considerations

9.15.1 Certain child protection concerns which come to the attention of the health boards are of particular relevance to the An Garda Síochána.

Age of Consent

9.15.2 For the purposes of the criminal law, the age of consent to sexual activity is **17 years**. This means, for example, that a sexual relationship between two 16 year olds who are boyfriend and girlfriend is illegal, although it might not be regarded as constituting child sexual abuse. **In any event, investigations should be sensitive to the needs of the child.** Where abuse is suspected, early advice should be sought from the Director of Public Prosecutions by an Garda Síochána

9.15.3 In cases where abuse is not suspected or alleged, but the boy or girl is under age, consultation must be held between the health board and An Garda Síochána who will examine all aspects of the case. Both agencies must acknowledge the sensitivity required in order to facilitate vulnerable young people in availing of all necessary services while at the same time satisfying relevant legal requirements.

Under-Age Pregnancy

9.15.4 When a pregnant girl under 17 years presents to a health service, a health professional will undertake an assessment and attempt to establish whether this pregnancy is the result of child sexual abuse. Two key issues will be considered:

> (i) the presence or otherwise of evidence to suggest child sexual abuse;
>
> (ii) whether any previous report or notification has been made to the health board concerning the girl or her family.

9.15.5 In cases where abuse is suspected or alleged, the Child Care Manager/designate must be informed, using the Standard Notification Form (Appendix Eight), and a Notification made to An Garda Síochána (see **Form 9.1** at the end of this chapter).

9.15.6 In cases where abuse is not suspected or alleged, local health board procedures should be in place to provide guidance on consultation with An Garda Síochána to examine all aspects of these cases. **Agencies must acknowledge the sensitivity required in order to facilitate vulnerable young girls to avail of medical or therapeutic services and to satisfy relevant legal requirements.**

Retrospective Disclosure by Adults

9.15.7 When a disclosure is made by an adult of abuse suffered during their childhood and it comes to the attention of either the health board or An Garda Síochána or other service, serious consideration must be given to the current risk to any child who may be in contact with the alleged abuser. If any risk is deemed to exist, this information must be shared between agencies, following the notification procedures. The need to refer an adult for counselling, treatment and/or other support services for victims of assaults should be considered. **It is essential that all relevant information in relation to any of the above eventualities is carefully collated and that each agency informs the other of any such concerns during an investigation.**

9.16 Arrangements for the Protection of Children At Risk Whose Families Move to another Jurisdiction

9.16.1 When a family with children who are considered by the health board or An Garda Síochána to be at risk are believed to have moved to another jurisdiction, the relevant information should be sent to the appropriate authority in that State. The procedures to be followed are outlined in **Appendix Nine.**

9.17 Arrangements for the Protection of Children At Risk Who Migrate to Ireland from Another Jurisdiction

9.17.1 When the health board or An Garda Síochána are informed that a child or children who are considered to be at risk have moved into their area, immediate notification procedures must be followed. If required, a strategy meeting must be arranged between the health board and An Garda Síochána to review relevant information.

FORM 9.1

STANDARD NOTIFICATION FORM

FOR USE BY HEALTH BOARDS IN NOTIFYING CASES

TO AN GARDA SIOCHANA

<u>CONFIDENTIAL</u>

_____ Health Board

_____ Address

To: Superintendent
      Garda Síochána
      Address _____ Ref. No. _____

NOTIFICATION OF SUSPECTED CHILD ABUSE

Child's Name _____

D.O.B. _____ Sex _____

Address _____

Father's Name _____ Mother's Name _____

1. The above named child has come to notice as a possible victim of child abuse.

2. Form(s) of abuse suspected (see overleaf):

     ❏ Neglect   ❏ Physical Abuse   ❏ Emotional Abuse*   ❏ Sexual Abuse

     *All abuse involves an element of emotional ill-treatment; this category should be used where it is the main or sole form of abuse suspected.

3. Additional information _____

_____

_____

The Social Worker dealing with this matter is:

Name _____

Phone No. _____

Address _____

Signed _____   Date _____
        Designated Officer

Return Slip (to be returned to relevant Health Board)

Garda   Garda Ref. No.
Address: Child's Name:

I acknowledge receipt of your notification.
The Garda assigned to this case is:

Name _____   Phone No. _____

Address _____

                                                    Signed: _____

FORM 9.2

STANDARD NOTIFICATION FORM

FOR USE BY AN GARDA SIOCHANA IN NOTIFYING CASES

TO HEALTH BOARDS

<u>**CONFIDENTIAL**</u>

Garda Síochána   Ref. No. _____

_____ Address

To: Designated Officer

_____ Health Board

Address _____

NOTIFICATION OF SUSPECTED CHILD ABUSE

Child's Name _____

D.O.B. _____ Sex _____

Address _____

Father's Name _____ Mother's Name _____

1. The above named child has come to notice as a possible victim of child abuse.

2. Form(s) of abuse suspected (see overleaf):

   ❐ Neglect   ❐ Physical Abuse   ❐ Emotional Abuse*   ❐ Sexual Abuse

   *All abuse involves an element of emotional ill-treatment; this category should be used where it is the main or sole form of abuse suspected.

3. Additional information _____

_____

_____

The Garda dealing with this matter is:

Name _____

Phone No. _____

Address _____

Signed _____   Date _____
         Designated Officer

Return Slip (to be returned to relevant Garda Station)

Health Board   Health Board Ref. No.
Address: Child's Name:

I acknowledge receipt of your notification.
The Social Worker assigned to this case is:

Name _____   Phone No. _____

Address _____

                                                   Signed: _____

FORM 9.3

JOINT ACTION SHEET

CASE MANAGEMENT NOTE:

Notification No: Child's Name: Age:

Date Received: Address

Category Of Child Abuse?   Medical Examination Complete Yes/No

                       If yes: Details _____

CONTACT WITH HEALTH BOARD/GARDAI ESTABLISHED?

STRATEGY MEETING — DATE HELD:

DETAILS OF CASE PLAN

Decisions for Action:

LIAISON MANAGEMENT MEETING — DATE HELD:

Details of Review

Decision for Action:

FURTHER COMMENTS:

D.P.P. DECISION   CHARGE(S):

COURT DATE: OUTCOME:

CASE CLOSURE — DATE:

Signed: _____   _____
             Garda   Social Worker

           _____   _____
            Garda Inspector/Sergeant   Social Work Team Leader

Special Considerations

part four

10 Specially Vulnerable Children & Abuse Outside the Home

10.1 Purpose

10.1.1 This chapter provides additional guidance concerning children who may be especially vulnerable and children outside the home. The procedures to be followed where homeless children may have been abused are detailed. Finally, the chapter deals with extra-familial abuse and the issues which arise in the investigation of organised child abuse.

10.2 Children with Disabilities

10.2.1 Children with disabilities may be more at risk of abuse for the following reasons:

    (i) communication difficulties;

    (ii) sensory disabilities;

    (iii) vulnerability due to isolation;

    (iv) dependence on goodwill of carers;

    (v) power differences;

    (vi) limited assertiveness;

    (vii) limited ability to recognise inappropriate sexual behaviour;

    (viii) need for intimate care such as washing and toileting;

    (ix) contact with multiple care services and carers;

    (x) frequent staff turnover;

    (xi) compliant behaviour towards adults;

    (xii) limited understanding of sexuality or sexual behaviour;

    (xiii) need for attention, friendship or affection;

    (xiv) limited sense of danger and inability to see warning signs;

    (xv) fear of not being believed;

    (xvi) perceived limited reliability as witnesses.

10.2.2 Research has shown that abuse of children with disabilities is a significant problem. The abusers are most likely to be known to the victim. Parents, teachers and all staff in services for children with disabilities need to be familiar with the indicators of abuse and to be alert for signs of abuse. All agencies working with children with disabilities should have clear guidelines for preventing, identifying and reporting child abuse and should ensure that staff and volunteers are trained in the use of these National Guidelines.

10.3   Homeless Children

10.3.1   Occasionally, children will come to the attention of the health board whose circumstances are unclear and who, because of what may be temporary difficulties, are without accommodation. In such circumstances the following actions should be taken:

10.3.2   Establish with the child, in a manner which is appropriate to his or her age and stage of development, the circumstances in which (s)he became homeless.

10.3.3   As soon as possible, contact the child's parents/carers, establish their circumstances and their view of the situation.

10.3.4   Make an assessment of any possible risks constituted by re-uniting the child with his or her parents.

10.3.5   If it is considered to be in the child's best interests to return to his or her parents/carers, establish whether the parents/carers are willing and able to take the child back.

10.3.6   Talk with the child and see if (s)he is willing to return to his or her carer/s.

10.3.7   If a return to the child's parents/carers is not considered the most appropriate action, talk with both the child and the parents/carers to try to identify an alternative temporary placement with a family member or friend which is acceptable to the parents/carers and the child and agreed by them.

10.3.8   If the child's parents/carers cannot be contacted, the health board is obliged to take such steps as are reasonable to offer the child accommodation, pending further assessment.

10.3.9   Where it is not possible to return a homeless child to his or her parents/carers or to find a temporary placement with relatives or friends, then the health board has three options:

> (i)   If circumstances warrant, the health board may pursue an Emergency Care Order.
>
> (ii)   There may be a voluntary reception of the child into the care of the health board.
>
> (iii)   If grounds for receiving the child into care are not clear or do not exist and there appears to be no suitable accommodation for the child, then the health board has an obligation to provide him or her with a place to stay which is suitable to his or her needs. This placement should be short term, pending a full assessment.

10.3.10 Any concern about the care and protection of a homeless child should be assessed in the same way as any other child protection concern. Many homeless children present outside normal office house and all health boards should operate an out-of hours service in order to meet their needs.

10.4 Children in Foster Care

10.4.1 Health boards have responsibilities for children whom they place with foster parents. In arranging, providing or supervising placements with foster parents, the welfare of the child must be paramount. The wishes and feelings of the child and their parents should be taken into account.

10.4.2 Some children entering foster care may have previously been abused. Any allegation of abuse must be dealt with sensitively and support provided to the child, the foster carers and their family.

10.4.3 When the health board is investigating alleged abuse of foster children, the safety of any other children in the household should be considered. Article 22 of The Child Care (Placement of Children in Foster Care) Regulations 1995 gives a health board power to terminate foster care placements where considered appropriate.

10.5 Children in Residential Settings

10.5.1 All those involved in caring for children in residential settings, including schools, must be alert to the possibility of abuse by other children, visitors and members of staff. Policies and procedures aimed at preventing abuse must be in place. There must be clear written procedures on how to deal with suspected abuse. These must be accessible to children and staff.

10.5.2 When a child has been abused by another child in the home or school, child protection procedures should be applied to both the abuser and the victim.

10.6 Role of the Health Board

10.6.1 Under the Child Care Act, 1991 the health board is required to assume primary responsibility for an assessment and to take appropriate steps to protect the welfare of the child or children in question. In practice this means that the Child Care Manager/designate co-ordinates the services necessary to identify whether a particular child or children need of care or protection and, if so, initiate appropriate action. In doing this the Child Care Manager/designate will liaise closely with and, where required, enlist the assistance of the referring service.

10.7 Steps to be Taken if Abuse is Suspected

10.7.1 An employee of a service for children with disabilities or a member of the public who comes in contact with that service, who suspects that abuse may be taking place should follow the general procedures regarding reporting to the health board (see Chapter Four).

10.8 Safeguarding Children

10.8.1 Children in residential settings should have contact with people outside the home or school. These children are particularly vulnerable and may find it very difficult to make their problems known. The following measures should be in place in all residential settings for children:

(i) children should be told about the complaints system;

(ii) children should have contact cards which ensure an urgent response from senior management;

(iii) children should have easy access to a telephone where they can speak privately;

(iv) children should be made aware of telephone helpline numbers;

(v) approved visitors from outside the home should be available to see the children.

10.8.2 Health boards and the Social Services Inspectorate have a duty to visit children in various residential settings and they should ensure that each facility has child protection procedures in place.

10.9 Abuse by Visitors

10.9.1 The possibility of abuse by visitors must be recognised. If such abuse occurs, it should normally be dealt with in the same way as other incidents of suspected abuse.

10.10 Abuse by Staff

10.10.1 Children and staff must be able to report their concerns. There should be clear written guidance on reporting suspected abuse. The need to be vigilant and to report concerns should be reinforced through training and supervision.

10.10.2 Both children and staff need to be reassured that raising concerns is important. Management should react to all reports of a concern quickly and appropriately, and ensure that effective action is taken. A written record of the report should be confirmed with the reporter.

10.10.3 Throughout the investigation all interviews with children should be pre-arranged and they should be provided with the following:

(i) support;

(ii) information about the investigation and its outcome;

(iii) privacy in interviewing and in access to the telephone and correspondence;

(iv) access to independent advice if required;

(v) alternative accommodation if required.

10.10.4 There should be clear procedures on what the child or member of staff should do if they feel that inappropriate or insufficient action has been taken.

10.10.5 Where abuse by a member of staff is suspected, normal child protection procedures should be instigated. The investigation should be carried out by a senior member of the health board's staff who does not have immediate line management responsibility for the home and should include an independent person. Staff and management should co-operate fully with the investigation. The possibility of involvement and collusion of other members of staff must be recognised. Where such abuse is suspected, it will be necessary for An Garda Síochána and senior staff from the health board, when agreeing their strategy for investigation, to weigh the need for evidence carefully against the rights of the individual children concerned. Guidance on dealing with organised abuse is detailed later in this chapter (see 10.13).

10.11 Suspected Abuse in a Voluntary Organisation

10.11.1 Voluntary organisations working with children must be aware of the need to adopt child protection practices and to have in place procedures for dealing with suspected abuse.

10.11.2 Health boards should designate a social worker to act as liaison officer with voluntary and community organisations and to provide advice on child protection issues. Voluntary and community organisations should also be included in relevant training courses.

10.11.3 Where organisations suspect a member of staff or volunteer of abuse they should inform the health board who will begin child protection procedures. The organisation should notify the health board of any other organisations working with children with which the alleged abuser is thought to be involved. The health board should include these organisations in any investigation, if appropriate.

10.12 Extra-Familial Abuse

10.12.1 Abuse may be carried out by someone other than an adult living in the immediate family. This may happen where the child is in contact with a member of the extended family, a friend, an acquaintance or a person whose professional activity brings them into contact with the child. Such abuse should be reported in the same way as intra-familial abuse.

10.13 Organised Abuse

10.13.1 Cases of organised abuse comprise only a very small proportion of the child protection concerns which come to the attention of health boards. Nevertheless, they are complex and require particularly careful handling. Essentially, organised abuse occurs when either one person moves into an area or institution and systematically entraps children for abusive purposes (mainly sexually) or when two or more adults conspire to similarly abuse children, using inducements.

10.13.2 Organised abuse can occur in different settings such as the community, the family or extended family or an institution.

10.13.3 The following factors are particularly associated with organised abuse:

(i) Detection can take several years.

(ii) Calculating the number of victims involved can be difficult as many will have moved away from the area. Particular efforts, such as help lines and advertisements, may be required in order to contact victims.

(iii) Victims are often more powerless and vulnerable than those in other abuse cases. Many will have grown up in care.

(iv) Victims may be under particular pressure not to disclose, because of threats or feelings of shame and responsibility.

(v) Some victims may have colluded with abusers to entrap other children and may have gone on to become abusers themselves.

(vi) Families may have unwittingly colluded with the abuse by accepting gifts and friendship from the abuser and encouraging their children to associate with the abuser.

10.13.4 The investigation of organised abuse requires particularly sensitive co-operation between health boards and An Garda Síochána. It may involve surveillance work, and a higher degree of secrecy than would normally be expected in child protection work. It may be undesirable to share information fully with families in the early stages of investigation since breaches of confidentiality may seriously impede detection.

11 *Peer Abuse*

9.1 Purpose

11.1.1 In some cases of child abuse the alleged perpetrator will also be a child. In such situations, it is particularly important to consider how a health board and other agencies can provide care for both the child victim and the child abuser. The purpose of this chapter is to provide guidance in regard to the management of such cases.

11.2 General Guidelines

11.2.1 In a situation where child abuse is alleged to have been carried out by another child, the child protection procedures should be adhered to for both the victim and the alleged abuser; that is, it should be considered a child care and protection issue for both children.

11.2.2 All abusers must be held accountable for their behaviour and work must be done to ensure that abusers take responsibility for their behaviour and acknowledge that the behaviour is unacceptable.

11.2.3 If there is any conflict of interest between the welfare of the alleged abuser and the victim, the victim's welfare is of paramount importance.

11.2.4 Abusive behaviour which is perpetrated by children must be taken seriously and it is important that such cases are referred to the health board. It is known that some adult abusers begin abusing during childhood and adolescence, that significant numbers will have suffered abuse themselves and that the abuse is likely to become progressively more serious. Early referral and intervention is therefore essential.

11.2.5 Children who are abusive towards other children require comprehensive assessment and therapeutic intervention by skilled child care professionals. Treatment is more likely to be effective if begun early in the child's life.

11.3 Sexual Abuse by Children and Young People

11.3.1 Research shows that one third of child sexual abuse in the Republic of Ireland is perpetrated by teenagers. Obviously it is important that behaviour of this nature is not ignored and cases should be referred to the health board. However it is also very important that the different types of behaviour are clearly identified and that no young person is wrongly labelled "a child abuser", without a clear analysis of the particular behaviour. One can identify four categories of behaviour which would warrant attention: normal sexual exploration; abuse reactive behaviour; sexually obsessive behaviour; abusive behaviour by adolescents and young people.

11.3.2 **Normal Sexual Exploration:** This could consist of naive play between two children which involves the exploration of their sexuality. This type of behaviour may be prompted by exchanges between children such as: "you show me yours and I'll show you mine". One of the key aspects of this behaviour is the tone of it. There should not be any coercive or dominating aspects to this behaviour. Usually, there is no need for child protection intervention of any kind in this type of situation.

11.3.3 **Abuse Reactive Behaviour:** In this situation, one child who has been abused already, acts out the same behaviour on another child. While this is serious behaviour and needs to be treated as such, the emphasis should be on addressing the victim needs of the child perpetrator.

11.3.4 **Sexually Obsessive Behaviour:** In this type of situation the children may engage in sexually compulsive behaviour. An example of this would be excessive masturbation which may well be meeting some other emotional need. Most children masturbate at some point in their lives. However, where children are in care or in families where care and attention is missing, they may have extreme comfort needs that are not being met and may move from masturbation to excessive interest or curiosity in sex, which takes on excessive or compulsive aspects. These children may not have been sexually abused but they may be extremely needy and may need very specific help in addressing these needs.

11.3.5 **Abusive Behaviour by Adolescents and Young People:** Behaviour that is abusive will have elements of domination, coercion or bribery and certainly secrecy. The fact that the behaviour is carried out by an adolescent, for example does not, in itself, make it "experimentation". However, if there is no age difference between the two children or no difference in status, power or intellect, then one could argue that this is indeed experimentation. On the other hand, if the adolescent is aged thirteen and the child is aged three, this gap in itself creates an abusive quality which should be taken seriously.

11.4   Treatment Services for Victims

11.4.1 As in all cases of child abuse, it is essential to respond to the needs of the children who are abused by their peers. Each category of child abuse may have different dynamics and effects. There is no single approach to the treatment of child abuse so each individual case will require its own unique intervention. Appropriate support and services should be provided to the child and his or her parents/carers as quickly as possible.

11.4.2 In the case of child sexual abuse, treatment approaches may include individual treatment and/or group therapy for the child or adolescent. Individual treatment allows the child/adolescent the opportunity to give his/her account of the abuse; talking about the abusive experience can often be an important first step. Group therapy offers the child/adolescent a supportive setting and an opportunity to address his or her sense of isolation and secrecy.

11.5 Prevention

11.5.1 There is a high probability that future abuse can be prevented if early intervention takes place. Treatment is more likely to be effective if begun early in the child's life. Therefore it is essential to refer concerns about peer abuse immediately to the relevant health board. Health boards should establish appropriate treatment programmes to cater for children who engage in abusive behaviour with other children.

11.6 Impact of Allegation on Child and Family

11.6.1 It should be anticipated that an allegation of abuse will have a detrimental impact on relationships between the alleged abuser, his parents and other family members. A negative impact on other social relationships such as with peers and neighbours should also be anticipated. As a result, the child and his family may experience isolation and in some situations victimisation following an allegation of abuse. The child's parents will need support and advice to help them understand the abusive behaviour and to deal with the situation. Active participation and commitment by parents can be an important factor in the success of treatment and may be crucial in influencing the general outcome of the case. It is therefore essential to provide adequate support services to the child and his family throughout the assessment and treatment processes.

11.7 Bullying

11.7.1 It is recognised that bullying in school is an increasing problem. It is imperative that school management boards should have in place a policy to deal with bullying, and that teachers are aware of this policy and of procedural guidelines to deal with bullying. In situations where the incident is serious and where the behaviour is regarded as potentially abusive, the school should consult the relevant health board with a view to drawing up an appropriate response such as a management plan.

11.7.2 Bullying can be defined as repeated aggression be it verbal, psychological or physical which is conducted by an individual or group against others. It is behaviour which is intentionally aggravating and intimidating and occurs mainly among children in social environments such as schools. It includes behaviours such as teasing, taunting, threatening, hitting or extortion by one or more pupils against a victim. The more extreme forms of bullying behaviour, when perpetrated by adults rather than children, would be regarded as physical or emotional abuse. However other major forms of child abuse such as neglect and sexual abuse are not normally comprehended by the term bullying.

11.7.3 A module on child abuse, including bullying behaviour, should be included in the pre-service programmes for the professional training of teachers. The provision of in-career development courses for serving teachers would be of considerable benefit in raising awareness and developing techniques for dealing with such behaviour.

11.7.4 In the first instance it is the school authorities who are responsible for dealing with bullying in school. School authorities should exercise this responsibility having regard to the *Guidelines on Countering Bullying Behaviour in Primary and Post-Primary Schools* which were issued by the then Department of Education in 1993. School authorities should also take account of the *Child Abuse Prevention Programme* which was issued to all national schools under the joint auspices of the Departments of Education and Health in 1993; this programme covers all forms of child abuse including bullying. Only serious instances of bullying behaviour should be referred to the health board.

12 Allegations of Abuse Against Employees and Volunteers

12.1 Purpose

12.1.1 This chapter provides guidance to employers in a situation where an allegation of abuse is made against an employee. In this context, employees also include unpaid volunteers as well as foster-parents. Employers may encompass disability organisations, schools, crèches or non-governmental organisations such as sports clubs. The guidelines are offered to assist managers in having due regard for the rights and interests of the child on the one hand and those of the employee against whom the allegation is made on the other hand. Employers have a dual responsibility in respect of both the child and the employee. All employers should have agreed procedures to address situations where allegations of child abuse are made against an employee.

12.2 General Procedures

12.2.1 It is important to note that there are two procedures to be followed here:

> (i) the reporting procedure in respect of the child;
>
> (ii) the procedure for dealing with the employee.

In general it is recommended that the same person should not have responsibility for dealing with both the reporting issues and the employment issues. It is preferable to separate these issues and manage them independently. These procedures should be followed in the event of suspicion or disclosure of abuse against an employee.

12.2.2 Staff/volunteers may be subjected to erroneous or malicious allegations. Therefore any allegation of abuse should be dealt with sensitively and support provided for staff including counselling where necessary. However, the primary goal is to protect the child while taking care to treat the employee fairly.

12.3 Guidance on Reporting

12.3.1 **All organisations providing services to children should have clear written procedures on the action to be taken if allegations of abuse against employees are received.** Guidance should be provided for both children and staff/volunteers on how to report suspected abuse. The need for awareness and to report concerns should be reinforced through training and supervision.

12.3.2 Employers should ensure that children and staff are aware of internal line management reporting procedures. Employees should also be aware of the appropriate authorities to whom they should report *outside* the organisation if they are inhibited for any reason in reporting the incident internally or where they are dissatisfied with the internal response.

12.4 Employer's Responsibility to Report to Statutory Authorities

12.4.1 Where an employer becomes aware of an allegation of abuse by an employee the standard procedure for reporting allegations to the health board should be followed without delay (see Chapter Four). Health Boards should have their own internal reporting procedures in place in regard to allegations made against their employees.

12.4.2 Action taken in reporting an allegation of child abuse against an employee should be based on an opinion formed reasonably and in good faith. When an allegation is received it should be assessed promptly and carefully. It will be necessary to decide whether a formal report should be made to the health board; this decision should be based on reasonable grounds for concern as outlined in Chapter Four.

12.4.3 When an employer becomes aware of an allegation of abuse of a child or children by an employee during the execution of that employee's duties, the employer should privately inform the employee of the following:

> (i) the fact that an allegation has been made against him/her;
>
> (ii) the nature of the allegation.

The employee should be afforded an opportunity to respond. The employer should note the response and pass on this information when making the formal report to the health board.

12.4.4 Organisations as well as individuals may avail of the immunity from civil liability provided in the Protections for Persons Reporting Child Abuse Act, 1998 provided they report "reasonably and in good faith" to the appropriate authorities. Section 3(1) of the Act states:

> "3. (1) A person who, apart from this section, would be so liable shall not be liable in damages in respect of the communication, whether in writing or otherwise, by him or her to an appropriate person of his or her opinion that
>
> > (a) a child has been or is being assaulted, ill-treated, neglected or sexually abused, or
> >
> > (b) a child's health, development or welfare has been or is being avoidably impaired or neglected,
>
> unless it is proved that he or she has not acted reasonably and in good faith in forming that opinion and communicating it to the appropriate person".

12.5 Procedures for Dealing with Employees and Employer's Duty of Care to Children

12.5.1 When an allegation is made against an employee, the following steps should be taken:

(i) Action should be guided by the agreed procedures, the applicable employment contract and the rules of natural justice.

(ii) The Chairperson (or equivalent head of organisation) should be informed as soon as possible.

(iii) The first priority should be to ensure that no child is exposed to unnecessary risk. The employer should as a matter of urgency take any necessary protective measures. These measures should be proportionate to the level of risk and should not unreasonably penalise the employee, financially or otherwise, unless necessary to protect children. Where protective measures do penalise the employee, it is important that early consideration be given to the case.

(iv) The follow up on an allegation of abuse against an employee should be made in consultation with the health board and An Garda Síochána. An immediate meeting should be arranged with these two agencies for this purpose.

(v) After these consultations referred to above and when pursuing the question of the future position of the employee, the Chairperson (or equivalent head of organisation) should advise the person accused of the allegation and the agreed procedures should be followed.

(vi) Employers/managers should take care to ensure actions taken by them do not undermine or frustrate any investigations being conducted by the health board or An Garda Síochána. It is strongly recommended that employers maintain a close liaison with these authorities to achieve this.

12.6 Guidance for Health Boards

12.6.1 Health boards will regularly receive allegations of abuse against people who have contact with children in their workplace or in a sports or youth club. If the health board considers that children are, or may be, at risk from the alleged abuser, they should contact the institution or employer immediately. In this situation it is not necessary to notify the alleged abuser in advance of the allegations against him or her.

12.6.2 Where a health board proposes to notify an alleged abuser's employer or person-in-charge of a club where (s)he attends, and where there is no immediate danger to children, the alleged abuser must be notified in advance of the allegations against him/her. The approach to an employer/person-in-charge in such cases may take place at any stage in the wider investigation and it may be practical that such an approach does not take place until any criminal or health board investigation has concluded.

12.6.3 Health boards should put arrangements in place to provide feedback to employers/persons-in-charge in regard to the progress of a child abuse investigation involving an employee. Efforts should be made by health boards to investigate complaints against employees promptly and to complete their assessment as quickly as possible bearing in mind the serious implications for the innocent employee. Employers/persons-in-charge should be notified of the outcome of an investigation. The health board should pass on reports and records to the employer and to the employee in question where appropriate. This will assist the employer/person-in-charge in reaching a decision as to the action to be taken in the longer term concerning the employee.

Local Arrangements

part five

13 Support Services to Children and Families

13.1 Purpose

13.1.1 This chapter identifies some of the key sources of stress in child protection work and offers guidance on how to address them. The chapter also offers guidance on how to ensure personal safety in child protection work.

13.2 Sources of Stress in Child Protection Work

13.2.1 Child protection work, by its nature, can provoke high stress levels at certain times. The sources of stress include the following:

   (i) distressing nature of certain abusive incidents or circumstances;

   (ii) need to judge levels of risk and take decisions quickly;

   (iii) need to balance children's safety and rights and privacy of parents/carers;

   (iv) scarcity of appropriate resources when needed;

   (v) heavy caseloads;

   (vi) staff shortages;

   (vii) lack of support for practitioners;

   (viii) inter-agency and inter professionals tensions.

13.2.2 It is essential that managers of all disciplines involved in child protection acknowledge the levels of actual or potential stress that may affect their staff, and take steps to address the problem. These steps may include the following:

   (i) adequate and regular supervision of staff;

   (ii) regular review of caseloads;

   (iii) acknowledgement of positive achievement;

   (iv) provision of opportunities for professional development such as training, staff rotation, special assignments;

   (v) development of inter agency links.

13.3 Personal Safety in Child Protection Work

13.3.1 Child protection work occasionally brings staff into situations which may present risks to their physical and psychological safety. Apart from the real likelihood in some circumstances of personal injury or serious trauma, the prospect of a frightening encounter can profoundly affect a worker's capacity to make sound decisions in a case. **It is essential that employers and line managers recognise that stress and anxiety in such circumstances is a legitimate reaction, and not a sign of personal weakness or lack of professionalism.**

13.3.2 Measures which can alleviate or combat threats to the safety of staff can include the following:

> (i) security arrangements in health centres and other work sites, such as the presence of a porter or other security staff;
>
> (ii) 'filtering' of telephone and personal callers;
>
> (iii) a system whereby the location of staff is known at all times;
>
> (iv) adequate protection if a proposed meeting or encounter seems likely to elicit a hostile or aggressive response;
>
> (v) while the responsibility for staff safety ultimately rests with employers, staff themselves must be responsible about bringing a potentially risky situation to the attention of their line manager.

13.3.3 If a staff member is subject to any type of assault or personal attack, or is subjected to a traumatic experience in the course of their professional duties, employers must acknowledge the gravity of what has occurred and take whatever steps are necessary to support the worker and reduce the possibility of recurrence.

14 Training in Child Protection

14.1 Purpose

14.1.1 The purpose of this chapter is to outline the role of training for effective child protection and the levels of training required for different types of staff in all organisations working with children. One of the core issues identified in child abuse enquiries is the breakdown in communication between disciplines and agencies in cases of child abuse. Accordingly it is essential that training is provided on a multi-disciplinary, inter-agency basis.

14.1.1 Training aims to promote effective interventions in the care and protection of children. Effective child protection depends on the skills, knowledge and values of personnel working with children and families as well as intra-agency and inter-agency co-operation. Relevant training and education is an essential pre-requisite to achieving this. All agencies involved with children have a responsibility to ensure that such training is available on an ongoing basis.

14.2 Objectives of Child Protection Training

Training in child protection has a number of objectives as follows:

(i) to ensure that personnel are equipped with appropriate skills, knowledge and values to deliver an effective service to children;

(ii) to ensure that personnel are aware of relevant legislation, national guidelines and local child protection procedures and protocols;

(iii) to translate learning into a better service for children and families in collaboration with other service providers;

(iv) to strengthen relationships through inter-agency training.

14.3 Approach to Child Protection Training

14.3.1 The level and type of training required depends on the degree of involvement that the staff of particular agencies have in child protection work. All relevant staff should be trained in the recognition of signs of abuse and what immediate action to take.

14.3.2 A strategy for training in child care and protection must be developed in each health board. This strategy will set out the training aims, learning outcomes, target groups, proposed initiatives, performance indicators and evaluation processes involved.

14.3.3 Training in child care and protection will need to be available at two levels — basic level and advanced level — in order to meet a diversity of needs within health boards and other agencies who provide services to children and families.

14.3.4 **Basic level training** in child care and protection should aim to equip personnel with a knowledge and skills on the relevant child care legislation, national and local agency policies, procedures and protocols as well as a knowledge of the local network within which they work. Basic level child care and protection training must be delivered on a multi-disciplinary inter-agency basis. The key learning that takes place results from multi-disciplinary and inter-agency discussion and the sharing of knowledge, experience and perspectives.

14.3.5 **Advanced level training** in child care and protection should aim to equip personnel with knowledge, skills and critical perspectives in specific areas of policy and practice, for example, risk assessment and working in partnership with parents/carers. Training should be appropriate to the person's professional role and should be delivered on a multi-disciplinary inter-agency basis.

14.4 Target Groups

14.4.1 There are two key target groups for training in child care and protection. The first is staff in the health boards and An Garda Síochána by virtue of their statutory responsibility for child protection. The second is staff in a wide range of agencies, both statutory and voluntary, who provide services to children and families and who have a social responsibility to safeguard the welfare of children. These include, inter alia, disability organisations, schools, pre-school services, sports clubs and other voluntary organisations.

14.4.2 Professionals who are key front line staff in child protection work such as social workers, public health nurses, medical doctors and An Garda Síochána, should have a module on the basics of child protection incorporated into their general professional training. Ongoing training in this area is essential for all such personnel; professionals themselves have a responsibility to see that they keep up to date with current developments in this area.

14.4.3 Appropriate training in child care and protection is needed for all social work staff in child care and child protection services, all residential care staff and all foster parents with whom health boards have placed children. Social work teams in each health board are encouraged to support the development of inter-agency and multi-disciplinary training for all staff engaged in child protection work and to provide places on their training courses for non-health board staff.

14.5 Training for Health Board Personnel

14.5.1 Child care and protection is a corporate responsibility of all employees of health boards. The development of training strategies at health board level must reflect this premise with appropriate training at a multi-disciplinary level.

14.5.2   The target group for basic level training in child care and protection should be personnel whose role involves direct or indirect contact with children and families.

14.5.3   The target group for advanced level training in child care and protection should be personnel whose core duties involve the supervision or practice of child protection and the provision of support services to children and families

14.6   Training for Staff in Other Agencies who Provide Services to Children and Families and who have a Social Responsibility to Safeguard the Welfare of Children

14.6.1   The Department of Health and Children, through the health boards, actively promotes inter-disciplinary and inter-agency co-operation in order to secure the welfare of children. This is an essential element in the professional task of protecting children from abuse. All agencies involved with children should participate in inter-agency training programmes.

14.6.2   All agencies should establish joint training programmes on child abuse issues with access for all professional groups in direct contact with children and families. These programmes, preferably involving trainers from a variety of relevant agencies, should help to promote understanding of the respective roles of staff in each agency and thus promote effective working relationships.

14.6.3   A designated senior staff member in each organisation should play a central role in developing and monitoring training in child care and protection under the auspices of the Child Protection Committee. This development should include co-operation across community care areas as well as between health boards. Staff in all relevant agencies should be made aware of any training opportunities which exist and be encouraged to participate.

14.6.4   The management of schools, pre-school services and voluntary organisations must also ensure that personnel are trained in the recognition of signs of abuse and on how to report it.

14.6.5   Front line personnel in such services who meet the public, like telephonists and receptionists, should be given clear instructions on what action to take if contacted by anyone wishing to report suspected child abuse.

14.7   Specialist Training

14.7.1   Specialist training is required for selected health board staff and members of An Garda Síochána who will be involved in the joint investigation of cases and subsequent intervention (see Chapter Nine). The aim of this training is to enable members of each service to understand fully each other's role, to learn how to work together on a joint basis, and to learn how to interview children who may have been abused by adults.

14.8 Evaluation

14.8.1 A designated senior staff member in each organisation should play a central role in developing, monitoring and evaluating training in child care and protection under the auspices of the Child Protection Committee. Training needs will change continuously and training in child care and protection must be an integral part of the plans in all agencies. A percentage of the annual budget in each agency should be explicitly committed to child protection training. An annual review of the training strategy for child care and protection should be undertaken.

15 Content and Format of Local Procedures and Guidance

15.1 Purpose

15.1.1 Statutory and voluntary/community organisations working with children should adapt these National Guidelines in order to make them as meaningful and effective as possible for their staff and volunteers. The content of local guidelines should not vary from the National Guidelines but there may be particular specificity or elaboration appropriate to local circumstances. Schools, hospitals and community organisations will need to outline specific procedures for personnel on how to respond to concerns or suspicions of child abuse. Where voluntary/community organisations wish to have their local guidelines reviewed for their efficacy, the health board in the area will facilitate this.

15.1.2 The purpose of local guidelines is to provide sufficient information to enable staff who work with children to be alert and aware about what to do in situations where child abuse may be a concern or suspicion and to facilitate personnel in using the procedures and structures to work co-operatively to protect children.

15.2 Local Procedures and Guidance

15.2.1 Local procedures and guidance, within the framework of the National Guidelines, should be developed by, inter alia:

(i) health boards, and made available to health board personnel and general practitioners;

(ii) hospitals;

(iii) mental health services;

(iv) education services, and made available to teaching and school personnel;

(v) probation and welfare services;

(vi) day care centres/pre-school services;

(vii) voluntary and community organisations.

15.2.2 The local guidelines should draw upon and localise the following elements of the National Guidelines:

(i) **Definitions and Reporting Procedure:** These should be adopted as per Chapters Three and Four of the National Guidelines. It is essential that there is consistency in regard to definitions, the basis for reporting and the standard reporting procedure. Guidance on confidentiality as per Chapter Five should also be adopted.

(ii) **Roles and Responsibilities:** Chapter Six of the National Guidelines should be supplemented by describing the roles of local agencies and arrangements for joint working and co-operation between them at local level.

(iii) **Individual and Corporate Responsibility:** Chapter Six of the National Guidelines should be referenced and specific direction given as to what is expected of individuals and organisations in regard to reporting concerns and participating in the child protection process.

(iv) **Assessment:** Part Three of the National Guidelines should be referenced in localised guidance for health board staff because it outlines the role of health board staff in assessing cases and the steps that are taken. Local arrangements for parental involvement and child participation should be described.

(v) **Key elements in the Child Protection Process:** Part Three of the National Guidelines should be modified as appropriate to provide sufficient and relevant information on what is involved in the child protection process once a concern or report is advised to the health board (assessment, child protection conferences, management of cases, case reviews, case closure). This should include advice on special circumstances as appropriate for example children with disabilities, children in foster care and residential settings, peer abuse.

(vi) **Allegations of Abuse Against Employees:** Chapter Twelve of the National Guidelines should be referenced and supplemented by agreed local procedures on the action to be taken when an allegation is made.

(vii) **Training:** Chapter Fourteen of the National Guidelines should be referenced. The local commitment and arrangements for training in regard to child protection should be described.

15.3 Introduction to Local Guidelines

An introduction to localised guidance should include a description of the aims and principles as per Chapter One of the National Guidelines.

15.4 Template for Local Guidelines

Each section of local guidance should provide:

(i) clear descriptions of responsibility at local level, both individual and corporate;

(ii) organisation and management arrangements as well as procedures for child protection, including arrangements for inter-agency co-operation;

(iii) expectations of best professional practice;

(iv) arrangements for training and support of staff;

(v) approach to family support and the involvement of the child.

Appendices

part six

Appendix 1 *Signs and Symptoms of Abuse*

1. Signs and Symptoms of Child Neglect

This category of abuse is the most common. A distinction can be made between "wilful" neglect and "circumstantial" neglect. For instance, "wilful" neglect would generally incorporate a direct and deliberate deprivation by a parent/carer of a child's most basic needs e.g. withdrawal of food, shelter, warmth, clothing, contact with others, whereas "circumstantial" neglect more often may be due to stress/inability to cope by parents or carers. Neglect is closely correlated with low socio-economic factors and corresponding physical deprivations. It is also related to parental incapacity due to learning disability or psychological disturbance.

The neglect of children is **"usually a passive form of abuse involving omission rather than acts of commission"**. It comprises **"both a lack of physical caretaking and supervision and a failure to fulfil the developmental needs of the child in terms of cognitive stimulation".**[*]

Child neglect should be suspected in cases of:

- Abandonment or desertion

- Children persistently being left alone without adequate care and supervision

- Malnourishment, lacking food, inappropriate food or erratic feeding

- Lack of warmth

- Lack of adequate clothing

- Lack of protection and exposure to danger including moral danger or lack of supervision appropriate to the child's age

- Persistent failure to attend school

- Non-organic failure to thrive i.e. child not gaining weight not alone due to malnutrition but also due to emotional deprivation

- Failure to provide adequate care for the child's medical problems

- Exploited, overworked

2. Signs and Symptoms of Emotional Child Abuse

Emotional abuse occurs when adults responsible for taking care of children are unable to be aware of and meet their children's emotional and developmental needs. Emotional abuse is not easy to recognise because the effects are not easily observable. **"Emotional abuse refers to the habitual verbal harassment of a child by disparagement, criticism, threat and ridicule and the**

---

[*] Skuse, D. and Bentovim, A. (1994) "Physical and Emotional Maltreatment". In Rutter, M. Taylor, E. and Hersor, L. (Editors), Child and Adolescent Psychiatry (Third Edition), Oxford: Blackwell Scientific Publications.

inversion of love; whereby verbal and non-verbal means of rejection and withdrawal are substituted."

Emotional abuse can be defined in reference to the following indices. However, it should be noted that no one indicator is conclusive of emotional abuse.

- Rejection

- Lack of praise and encouragement

- Lack of comfort and love

- Lack of attachment

- Lack of proper stimulation (e.g. fun and play)

- Lack of continuity of care (e.g. frequent moves)

- Serious over-protectiveness

- Inappropriate non-physical punishment (e.g. locking in bedrooms)

- Family conflicts and/or violence

- Every child who is abused sexually, physically or neglected is also emotionally abused

- Inappropriate expectations of a child's behaviour — relative to his/her age and stage of development.

3. Signs and Symptoms of Physical Abuse

Unsatisfactory explanations or varying explanations for the following events are highly suspicious:

- Bruises (see below for more detail)

- Fractures

- Swollen joints

- Burns/Scalds(see below for more detail)

- Abrasions/Lacerations

- Haemorrhages (retinal, subdural)

- Damage to body organs

- Poisonings — repeated (prescribed drugs, alcohol)

- Failure to thrive

- Coma/Unconsciousness

- Death.

** Skuse D. (1989) "Emotional Abuse and Neglect" in Meadow, R. "ABC of Child Abuse", British Medical Journal Publications, London.

There are many different forms of physical abuse but skin, mouth and bone injuries are the most common.

Bruises — in General

Accidental bruises are common at places on the body where bone is fairly close to the skin. Bruises can also be found towards the front of the body, as the child usually will fall forwards.

Accidental bruises are common on the chin, nose, forehead, elbow, knees and shins. An accident-prone child can have frequent bruises in these areas. Such bruises will be diffuse with no definite edges. Any bruising on a child before the age of mobility must be treated with concern.

Suspicion

Bruises are more likely to occur on soft tissues e.g. cheek, buttocks, lower back, back or thighs and calves, neck, genitalia and mouth.

Bruises — non-accidental

Marks from slapping or grabbing may form a distinctive pattern. Slap marks might occur on buttocks/cheeks and the outlining of fingers may be seen on any part of the body. Bruises may be associated with shaking which can cause serious hidden bleeding and bruising inside the skull. Any bruising around the neck is suspicious as it is very unlikely to be accidentally acquired. Bruises caused by direct blows with a fist have no definite pattern but may occur in parts of the body which do not usually receive injuries by accident. A punch over the eye (black eye syndrome) or ear would be of concern. Black eyes cannot be caused by a fall onto a flat surface. Two black eyes require two injuries and must always be suspect. Other injuries may feature — ruptured eardrum/fractured skull. Mouth injury may be a cause of concern — torn mouth (frenulum) from forced bottle-feeding. Other distinctive patterns of bruising may be left by the use of straps, belts, sticks and feet. The outline of the object may be left on the child in a bruise on areas such as back, thighs (areas covered by clothing).

Burns — in general

Children who have accidental burns usually have a hot liquid splashed on them by spilling or have come into contact with a hot object. The history that parents give is usually in keeping with the pattern of injury observed. However, repeated episodes may suggest inadequate care and attention to safety within the house.

Burns — non-accidental

Children who have received non-accidental burns may exhibit a pattern that is not adequately explained by parents. The child may have been immersed in a hot liquid. The burn may show a definite line, unlike the type seen in accidental splashing. The child may also have been held against a hot object like a radiator or a ring of a cooker leaving distinctive marks. Cigarette burns may result in multiple small lesions in places on the skin that would not generally be exposed to danger. There may be other skin conditions that can cause similar patterns and expert paediatric advice should be sought.

Bites — in general

Children can get bitten either by animals or humans. Animal bites, e.g. dogs — commonly puncture and tear the skin and usually the history is definite. Small children can also bite other children.

Bites — non accidental

It is sometimes hard to differentiate between adults' and childrens' bites as measurements can be inaccurate. Any suspected adult bite mark must be taken veryseriously. Consultant Paediatricians may liaise with Dental colleagues in order to correctly identify marks.

Bone injuries — in general

Children regularly have accidents that result in fractures. However, children's bones are more flexible than those of adults and the children themselves are lighter, so a fracture, particularly of the skull, usually signifies that considerable force has been applied.

Bone injuries — non-accidental

A fracture of any sort should be regarded as suspicious in a child under 8 months of age. A fracture of the skull must be regarded as particularly suspicious in a child under 3 years. Either case requires careful investigation as to the circumstances in which the fracture occurred. Swelling in the head or drowsiness may also indicate injury.

Poisoning — in general

Children may commonly take medicines or chemicals that are dangerous and potentially life threatening. Aspects of care and safety within the home need to be considered with each event.

Poisoning — non-accidental

Non-accidental poisoning can occur and may be difficult to identify but should be suspected in bizarre or recurrent episodes and when more than one child is involved. Drowsiness or hyperventilation may be a symptom.

Shaking violently

Shaking is a frequent cause of brain damage in very young children.

4. Signs and Symptoms of Child Sexual Abuse

Child sexual abuse often covers a wide spectrum of abusive activities. It rarely involves just a single incident and usually occurs over a number of years. Child sexual abuse frequently happens within the family. Intra-familial abuse is particularly complex and difficult to deal with.

Cases of sexual abuse principally come to light through:—

   (a) disclosure by the child or its siblings/friends;

   (b) the suspicions of an adult;

   (c) due to physical symptoms.

Colburn Faller*** provides a description of the wide spectrum of activities by adults which can constitute child sexual abuse. These include:

Non contact sexual abuse

- "Offensive Sexual Remarks" including statements the offender makes to the child regarding the child's sexual attributes, what he or she would like to do to the child and other sexual comments.
- Obscene Phone-calls
- Independent "exposure" involving the offender showing the victim his/her private parts and/or masturbating in front of the victim
- "Voyeurism" involving instances when the offender observes the victim in a state of undress or in activities that provide the offender with sexual gratification. These may include activities that others do not regard as even remotely sexually stimulating.

Sexual contact

- involving any touching of the intimate body parts. The offender may fondle or masturbate the victim and/or get the victim to fondle and/or masturbate them. Fondling can be either outside or inside clothes. Also includes "frottage", i.e. where offender gains sexual gratification from rubbing his/her genitals against the victim's body or clothing.

Oral-genital sexual abuse

- involving the offender licking, kissing, sucking or biting the child's genitals or inducing the child to do the same to them.

Interfemoral sexual abuse

- sometimes referred to as "dry sex" or "vulvar intercourse", involving the offender placing his penis between the child's thighs.

Penetrative sexual abuse of which there are four types

- "digital penetration" involving putting fingers in the vagina, or anus or both. Usually the victim is penetrated by the offender, but sometimes the offender gets the child to penetrate them.
- penetration with objects" involving penetration of the vagina, anus or occasionally mouth with an object.
- "genital penetration" involving the penis entering the vagina, sometimes partially.
- "anal penetration" involving the penis penetrating the anus.

*** Colbourn Faller, K. (1989) "Child Sexual Abuse". An Interdisciplinary Manual for Diagnosis Case Management and Treatment. Basingstoke: Macmillian.

Sexual exploitation

- Involves situations of sexual victimisation where the person who is responsible for the exploitation may not have direct sexual contact with the child. Two types of this abuse are child pornography and child prostitution.
- 'Child pornography' includes still photography, videos and movies and, more recently computer generated pornography.
- 'Child Prostitution' for the most part involves children of latency age or in adolescence. However, children as young as four and five are known to be abused in this way.
- Sexual abuse in combination with other abuse.
- The sexual abuses described above may be found in combination with other abuses, such as physical abuse and urination and defecation on the victim. In some cases physical abuse is an integral part of the sexual abuse; in others drugs and alcohol may be given to the victim.

It is important to note that physical signs may not be evident in cases of sexual abuse due to the nature of the abuse and/or the fact that the disclosure was made some time after the abuse took place.

Carers and professionals should be alert to the following physical and behavioural signs:—

- Bleeding from the vagina/anus
- Difficulty/pain in passing urine/faeces
- An infection may occur secondary to sexual abuse, which may or may not be a definitive sexually transmitted disease. Professionals should be informed if a child has a persistent vaginal discharge or has warts/rash in genital area.
- Noticeable and uncharacteristic change of behaviour
- Hints about sexual activity
- Age — inappropriate understanding of sexual behaviour
- Inappropriate seductive behaviour
- Sexually aggressive behaviour with others
- Uncharacteristic sexual play with peers/toys
- Unusual reluctance to join in normal activities which involve undressing, e.g. games/swimming

Particular behavioural signs and emotional problems suggestive of child abuse in young children (0-10 yrs):

- Mood change, e.g. child becomes withdrawn, fearful, acting out;
- Lack of concentration (change in school performance)
- Bed wetting, soiling
- Psychosomatic complaints; pains, headaches

- Skin disorders
- Nightmares, changes in sleep patterns
- School refusal
- Separation anxiety
- Loss of appetite
- Isolation

Particular behavioural signs and emotional problems suggestive of child abuse in older children (10 yrs +):

- Mood change, e.g. depression, failure to communicate
- Running away
- Drug, alcohol, solvent abuse
- Self mutilation
- Suicide attempts
- Delinquency
- Truancy
- Eating disorders
- Isolation

All signs/indicators need careful assessment relative to the child's circumstances.

Appendix 2 *Induced Illnesss (Munchausen Syndrome by Proxy)*

This is a condition where parents, usually the mother (according to current research and case experience), fabricate stories of illness about their child or substantiate the stories by causing physical signs e.g. by actively intervening in their child's medical treatment, by secretly administering dangerous drugs or other poisonous substances to their child or by smothering. Some of the warning signs of a parent fabricating a child's illness are:

(i) the illness is unexplained, despite extensive medical investigation, or extremely rare;

(ii) the symptoms and signs only occur in the presence of the parent;

(iii) the treatment prescribed is described as ineffective and not tolerated positively by the parent(s);

(iv) there are multiple illnesses and a history of similar symptoms in other family members;

(v) withdrawal of special treatment (e.g. naso-gastric feeds, IV lines) and "getting better", is not viewed with enthusiasm by the parents/carers.

This condition comprises a number of situations where significant harm may be caused to a child through impairment of that child's physical and emotional health and development, by parenting which:

(i) causes an illness state in the child by administration of noxious substances;

(ii) causes the child to have multiple (unnecessary) and at times dangerous, investigations because of the parent's belief that the child is ill;

(iii) leads to the child failing to thrive either through the active withholding of food or the giving of insufficient food.

Patterns Noted

The following patterns have been described:

1. **Active administration of a substance or active interference with the child's treatment or with the child**. Examples are children admitted to hospital following the active administration of substances e.g. un-prescribed medication, salt, laxatives; or where parents actively interfere with the child's medical treatment e.g. rubbing skin grafts, interfering actively with intravenous medication/feeding programme or where the parent specifically administers poison or smothers the child.

2. **Parents who allege their child has symptoms of a worrying nature**. Parents allege stopping breathing, fits, diarrhoea. Diagnoses such as apnoea, epilepsy or diabetes

insipidus are made on the basis of these reports and the child investigated and very possibly treated for them. When hospitalised the presenting symptoms are either fabricated actively by the parents or reported frequently, although never observed by medical and nursing staff, or nursing charts and medical tests may be interfered with by a parent.

3. **Failure to thrive through the active withholding of food**. This occurs in children who present with profound failure to thrive and severe developmental delay. Often, repeated statements have been made by the parents, especially the mother, that the child has been fed adequately but despite this, is not growing. Detailed close observation indicates a gross withholding of food from the child and/or disposing of the child's food.

4. **Alleged highly allergic children receiving insufficient amounts of food**. These children are often presented as being highly allergic to many different foods. Their diet therefore has been so severely restricted that they have received insufficient nutrition to grow. While there may be some organic basis to some allergic symptoms, it is not to the extent described by the parents.

In all such cases, when challenged the parents may disbelieve professional opinion and seek many further opinions.

Factors Associated With Such Presentations

1. The parent(s) have often held serious concerns about the child before/from birth, fears about his/her health and that the child might die. This may lead to concerns which go far beyond those which would be reasonable.

2. There may often have been paediatric concern about the child who may either have been treated as seriously symptomatic or whose illness presentation may be puzzling.

3. Parental anxiety often leads to fresh unexplained symptoms being presented, even after initial ones are treated or shown not to be serious or not to exist.

4. Children have often presented earlier in life with problems of failure to thrive, poor feeding and/or food allergies associated with maternal anxiety.

5. Family life seems to focus around the sick child at the point of referral. Current research suggests that mothers are responsible for the majority of inductions of illness or fictitious reporting. Some fathers actively support the mother's perception of the child as being ill, others are peripheral.

6. In hospital the parent shows intense involvement with the child, staying long hours at the bedside, often refusing to leave him/her or to let nursing staff carry out any care. There is intense and active involvement in all hospital processes. Frequently the mothers claim or actually have nursing or para-medical training.

7. Symptoms are observed and described when parents are present, and are not noted when the parents are absent.

8. Families have a high level of individual and family pathology e.g. long-term psychiatric problems, major marital problems, or a long-term history of privation and poor care. Somatisation and seeking medical support may be a solution to long-standing problems. Histories are often denied, difficult to elicit, and require considerable intensive investigation.

Management of Suspected Induced Illness

1. Managing initial suspicions and the identification of abuse is the task of the multi- disciplinary team involved with the health of the child. This requires an open-mindedness about the possibility of the illness being induced or fabricated.

2. An internal discussion must be convened to plan the identification.

3. A Consultant with expertise in this area must undertake and interpret the medical tests which clarify the nature of the illness perceived or induced by the family. Fabrication or induction of symptoms or illness state must be identified and distinguished from elements which may be due to physical processes.

4. On admission, detailed information must be gained about any medication or treatment the child is receiving, whom each element was prescribed by and confirmation gained from the named prescriber. A clear decision must be made and shared with the parents as to which medications the child will remain on during the admission. If new medications are prescribed while the child is an in-patient, similar clear decisions will be made.

5. An accurate account of the child's medical and developmental history, and of the parents medical, psychiatric and social history must be gained. Detailed information must be gained, both in writing and verbally by phone, from all medical personnel who have previously been involved with the child; e.g. GP, community and school doctors, paediatrician. This history gaining may immediately reveal significant discrepancies or an accumulation of concerns.

6. Detailed information about the child's functioning in school/nursery, both in the presence and absence of the parents, must be gained by the Social Worker.

7. If the family is known to the Health Board, detailed information should be gained.

8. The Social Worker will alert the Health Board to the suspicions after the Internal Discussion and keep them informed of any developments. If the suspicions of induced illness increase, Strategy Discussion(s) will be necessary to share information and to plan any protective action, including statutory action, which may be necessary in order to complete the initial assessment, even if the parents stop co-operating.

9. Medical tests, including collection of specimens, should be carried out without interference or intense involvement by the parents, unless an opportunity is being given for them to repeat patterns which have already been suspected and which need confirmation. Test results must be obtained from tests which could not have been tampered with.

10. Careful observation of the interaction between mother/child and other members of the family is essential as well as the child's interaction with ward staff. This may also show whether the child has been caught in the spiral of illness belief and behaviour. Detailed records must be kept in a confidential file.

11. Comprehensive assessment needs to be undertaken by the relevant members of the multi-disciplinary team, resulting in clear delineation of patterns in family life and individual functioning.

Discussion of Concerns with Parents

1. The Child Protection Teams in the Hospital and Health Board are responsible for planning and deciding when and how any concerns should be raised with the parents. It is essential that until suspicions are clearly proved, concerns should not be shared with the parents, because of the risk of their removing the child from Hospital without adequate protection. It can take time for evidence of parental interference to be identified and if the parents' suspicions are aroused they may remove the child before there is adequate evidence on which to base statutory action.

2. If a diagnosis of induced illness is confirmed, a Strategy Discussion must be held with the outside child protection and health agencies to plan the investigation and decide on the point at which the discussion of the concerns with the parents is undertaken. It is essential that there is a Child Protection Plan either in operation or ready to be used should the parents prove unco-operative.

3. Following the Strategy Discussion the usual child protection procedures will be followed, including not only the undertaking of any further investigation work but also the convening of an Initial Child Protection Conference, and the making of a detailed, long-term, multi-agency Treatment and Management Plan.

4. It should be noted that on occasions young people may fabricate symptoms themselves, without the knowledge of their parents. A similar diagnostic plan has to be made.

Appendix 3 *List of Health Board Addresses*

EASTERN HEALTH BOARD

REGIONAL DIRECTORS Child Care and Family Support Services		
Address	*Phone No.*	*Fax No.*
Dr Steeven's Hospital Dublin 8	01-6790700	01-6771523

AREA CHILD CARE MANAGER			
Community Care Area	*Address*	*Phone No.*	*Fax No.*
Area 1	Tivoli Road Dun Laoghaire, Co Dublin	01-2843579	01-2808785
Area 2	Vergemount Hall, Dublin 6	01-2698222	01-2830002
Area 3	The Malting Business Pk 54/55 Marrowbone Lane Dublin 8	01-4544826	01-4544827
Area 4	Old County Road Crumlin, Dublin 12	01-4542511	01-4542122
Area 5	The Lodge Cherry Orchard Ballyfermot, Dublin 10	01-6268101	01-6268281
Area 6	Rathdown Road, Dublin 7	01-8680444	01-8821208
Area 7	Aras Daibhin Jones's Road, Dublin 3	01-8552000	01-8554136
Area 8	Cromcastle Road Coolock, Dublin 5	01-8476122	01-8479944
Area 9	O'Donegans 4 New Road Newbridge Road, Naas Co Kildare	045-881974	045-881975
Area 10	Glenside Road, Wicklow	0404-68400	0404-69044

AREA SOCIAL WORK MANAGER

Community Care Area	Address	Phone No.	Fax No.
Area 1	Our Lady's Clinic Dun Laoghaire Co Dublin	01-2808403	01-2844955
Area 2	Vergemount Hall Dublin 6	01-2698222	01-2830002
Area 3	15 City Gate St Augustine St Dublin 8	01-6799296	01-6799303
Area 4	Old County Road Crumlin Dublin 12	01-4542511	01-4542122
Area 5	The Lodge Cherry Orchard Ballyfermot Dublin 10	01-6268101	01-6268281
Area 6	Rathdown Road Dublin 7	01-8680444	01-8680934
Area 7	Aras Daibhin Jones's Road Dublin 3	01-8552000	01-8554136
Area 8	Cromcastle Road Coolock Dublin 5	01-8476122	01-8479944
Area 9	Poplar House Poplar Square Naas Co Kildare	045-876001	045-879225
Area 10	Glenside Road Wicklow	0404-68400	0404-69044

MIDLAND HEALTH BOARD

REGIONAL DIRECTOR
Child Care and Family Support Services

Address	Phone No.	Fax No.
Primary Care Unit General Hospital Tullamore Co Offaly	0506-46283	0506-46226

AREA CHILD CARE MANAGER

Community Care Area	Address	Phone No.	Fax No.
Longford/ Westmeath	Health Centre Mullingar Co Westmeath	044-40221	044-39170
Laoise/Offaly	Health Centre Tullamore Co Offaly	0506-41301	0506-21136

AREA SOCIAL WORK MANAGER

Community Care Area	Address	Phone No.	Fax No.
Longford/ Westmeath	Health Centre Longford Co Longford	043-46211	043-46500
Laoise/ Offaly	O'Carroll St Tullamore Co Offaly	0506-22488	0506-21366

REGIONAL DIRECTOR Child Care and Family Support Services		
Address	Phone No.	Fax No.
87 O'Connell St Limerick	061-483592	061-317407

AREA CHILD CARE MANAGER			
Community Care Area	Address	Phone No.	Fax No.
Limerick	Vocational Training Services Dooradoyle Limerick	061-482792	061-482471
Clare	Tobartaoiscain Ennis Co Clare	065-23155 065-23156	065-43952
North Tipperary	General Hospital Nenagh Co Tipperary	067-31491	067-41357

AREA SOCIAL WORK MANAGER			
Community Care Area	Address	Phone No.	Fax No.
Limerick	Unit 3 St Camillus Hospital Shelbourne Rd Limerick	061-483711	061-483757
Clare	Tobartaoiscain Ennis Co Clare	065-23921	065-23926
North Tipperary	A.C.C. House Pearse St Nenagh Co Tipperary	067-31212	067-34334

REGIONAL DIRECTOR
Child Care and Family Support Services

Address	Phone No.	Fax No.
1st Floor Foley's Forge Dunshaughlin Co Meath	01-8250907	01-8250695

AREA CHILD CARE MANAGER

Community Care Area	Address	Phone No.	Fax No.
Cavan/ Monaghan	Health Care Unit Monaghan	047-30400	047-84587
Louth	Community Care Office Dublin Rd Dundalk Co Louth	042-9332287	042-9333814
Meath	Family Resource Centre Commons Road Navan Co Meath	046-73178	046-73183

AREA SOCIAL WORK MANAGER

Community Care Area	Address	Phone No.	Fax No.
Cavan/ Monaghan	Community Care Office Lisdarn Cavan	049-61822	049-61877
Louth	Community Care Office Dublin Road Dundalk	042-9332287	042-9333814
Meath	Child and Family Centre Navan Co Meath	046-21595	046-71377

NORTH-WESTERN HEALTH BOARD

AREA CHILD CARE MANAGER			
Community Care Area	*Address*	*Phone No.*	*Fax No.*
Donegal	Ballybofey Co Donegal	074-31391	074-31983
Sligo/ **Leitrim**	Markievicz House Sligo	071-55177	071-55131

AREA SOCIAL WORK MANAGER			
Community Care Area	*Address*	*Phone No.*	*Fax No.*
Donegal	County Clinic Letterkenny Co Donegal	Mobile: 087-2488181 074-22322	074-22592
Sligo/ **Leitrim**	Markievicz House Sligo	071-55133	071-55147

SOUTHERN HEALTH BOARD

AREA CHILD CARE MANAGER			
Community Care Area	*Address*	*Phone No.*	*Fax No.*
South Lee	Abbey Court House George's Quay, Cork	021-923814	021-963822
North Lee	Abbeycourt House Georges Quay Cork	021-965511	021-963822
North Cork	Hibernian Way Bank Place Mallow, Co Cork	021-30200	021-42504
West Cork	Hibernian Buildings Main St Skibbereen, Cork	028-23141	028-23172
Kerry	18 Denny St Tralee, Co Kerry	066-20300	066-81480

AREA SOCIAL WORK MANAGER

Community Care Area	Address	Phone No.	Fax No.
South Lee	Old Nurses Home St Finbarr's Hospital Douglas Road Cork	021-312525	021-312960
North Lee	**North Lee West** Floor 3 Abbeycourt House George's Quay Cork	021-965511	021-963822
	North Lee East Floor 4 Abbeycourt House George's Quay Cork	021-965511	021-963822
North Cork	Gouldshill House Mallow Co Cork	022-21484	022-42504
West Cork	West Cork Community Care Hospital Grounds Skibbereen Co Cork	028-21722	028-22382
Kerry	18-20 Denny St Tralee Co Kerry	066-23400	066-23407

SOUTH-EASTERN HEALTH BOARD

REGIONAL DIRECTOR
Child Care and Family Support Services

Address	Phone No.	Fax No.
Dublin Road Lacken Kilkenny	056-20400	056-52813

AREA CHILD CARE MANAGER

Community Care Area	Address	Phone No.	Fax No.
Carlow/Kilkenny	Community Care Centre James Green Kilkenny	056-52208	056-64172
Waterford	Community Care Centre Cork Road Waterford	051-842800	051-843688
Wexford	Community Care Centre Grogan's Road ACC Building George's St Wexford	053-65112 053-65113	053-23394
South Tipperary	Community Care Centre Western Rd Clonmel Co Tipperary	052-77000	052-25337

SOUTH-EASTERN HEALTH BOARD

AREA SOCIAL WORK MANAGER

Community Care Area	Address	Phone No.	Fax No.
Carlow/ Kilkenny	Patrick St Kilkenny	056-52208	056-62741
Waterford	Community Care Centre Cork Road Waterford	051-842800	051-843688
Wexford	South Eastern Health Board Ely House Wexford	053-47718 053-47719	053-47706
South Tipperary	Community Care Centre Western Road Clonmel Co Tipperary	052-22011	052-25337

WESTERN HEALTH BOARD

REGIONAL CO-ORDINATOR Child Care and Family Support Services		
Address	*Phone No.*	*Fax No.*
Child Care Unit Merlin Park Hospital Galway	091-757631	091-755632

AREA CHILD CARE MANAGER			
Community Care Area	*Address*	*Phone No.*	*Fax No.*
Galway	Community Care Offices 25 Newcastle Road Galway	091-523122 ext. 6228	091-524231
Mayo	Co Clinic Castlebar Co Mayo	094-22333 ext.2183	094-27106
Roscommon	HB Offices Lanesboro St Roscommon	0903-26732	0903-26732

AREA SOCIAL WORK MANAGER			
Community Care Area	*Address*	*Phone No.*	*Fax No.*
Galway	Community Care Offices 25 Newcastle Road Galway	091-523122 ext. 6330	091-527601
Mayo	Hill House Castlebar Co Mayo	094-22333	094-26110
Roscommon	Community Care Offices Ardsallagh Roscommon	0903-27089	0903-27043

Appendix 4 **Suggested Template for a Standard Reporting Form for Reporting Child Protection and Welfare Concerns to a Health Board**

1. Date of Report:

2. Name of person reporting:

3. Address of person reporting:

4. Relationship of reporting person with the child concerned

5. Method of Report (telephone call, personal call to office):

6. FAMILY DETAILS
   Details of child concerned

Surname
Forename
D.O.B.
Male/female
Alias (known as)
Address:

Correspondence address (if different)

Telephone number

7. State whether you consider your report to indicate (a) suspected or actual child abuse or (b) need for family support, giving reasons

	Physical Abuse	Sexual Abuse	Emotional Abuse	Neglect
Suspected	❏	❏	❏	❏
Actual	❏	❏	❏	❏

8. Details of other family members/household members

NAME	AGE	RELATIONSHIP TO CHILD	EMPLOYMENT/ SCHOOL	LOCATION

In cases of emergency, or outside health board hours, reports should be made to An Garda Síochána.

9. NAME OF OTHER PROFESSIONALS INVOLVED WITH CHILD/REN AND/OR PARENTS/ CARERS.

Public health nurse:

School:

General practitioner:

Any other agency or professional involved (please describe the nature of any involvement):

10. REPORT DETAILS

Describe, as fully as possible the nature of the problem or incident being reported, giving details of times and dates of individual incidents, the circumstances in which they occurred, any other persons who were present at the time, and their involvement:

11. Has any explanation been offered by the child, and/or parents/carers, which would account for the current problem or incident? (Details)

12. As far as possible, describe the state of the child/ren's physical, mental and emotional well-being

13. If child abuse is being alleged, who is believed to be responsible for causing it?

Include (if known)

Name:

Address:

Degree of contact with child:

Degree of contact with other children:

14. Describe (in detail) any risks to which the child/ren in this situation are believed to be exposed

15. How did this information come to your attention?

16. What has prompted you to report your concern at this time?

17. What <u>evidence</u> of harm exists at present?

18. Are there any factors in the child and/or parents/carers' present situation, which may have relevance to the current concern? (for example, recent illness, bereavement, separation, addiction, mental health problem or other difficulty)

19. Are there any factors in the child and/or parents/carers' situation which could be considered protective or helpful (for example, extended family or community support).

20. Has any action been taken in response to the current concern or incident/ (Details)

21. Are the child's parents/carers aware that this concern is being reported to the health board?

22. Is there a need for urgent protective action at this point?

23. Any other comments

SIGNED _____

DATE: _____

Appendix 5 *Terms of Reference for Regional and Local Child Protection Committees*

1. Principal Tasks of Regional Child Protection Committee

(i) to promote and review progress on arrangements to prevent child abuse;

(ii) to develop, monitor and review inter-agency and inter-professional child protection policies and procedures;

(iii) to monitor multi-disciplinary co-operation and bring any concerns to the local Child Protection Committees;

(iv) to identify the inter-disciplinary and inter-agency training needs and promote the development of an inter-disciplinary and inter-agency training strategy;

(v) to keep under review ways of raising public awareness of child abuse and mechanisms to express concerns about child abuse;

(vi) to initiate research on the prevention and treatment of child abuse;

(vii) to review significant issues arising from the handling of cases and reports from inquiries;

(viii) to develop a strategy for the provision of therapeutic services to perpetrators of abuse.

2. Principal Tasks of Local Child Protection Committee

(i) to monitor and review the implementation at community care level of arrangements to prevent child abuse;

(ii) to implement procedures and policies developed by the Regional Child Protection Committee for inter-agency and inter-professional co-operation at a local level;

(iii) to review the operation of inter-agency and inter-professional co-operation at a local level;

(iv) to provide a forum for a sharing of knowledge and experience by professionals on child protection at a local level;

(v) to keep under review ways of raising public awareness of child abuse and mechanisms to express concerns about child abuse at a local level.

Appendix 6 *Child Protection Conference Protocol*

1. Role of the Chairperson

The selection and training of child protection conference chairpersons is of particular importance. The main task of a chairperson **prior** to a conference is to ensure that:

(i) the holding of a conference is necessary;

(ii) the purpose of a conference is clear;

(iii) the relevant persons are invited and facilitated to attend, or enabled to contribute in some other manner;

(iv) the involvement of parents/carers and the child is appropriately managed;

(v) written reports are requested in advance from all professionals involved with the child and parents/carers in a relevant capacity, whether they are invited to the child protection conference or not;

(vi) adequate arrangements are in place regarding venue, recording arrangements and other structural requirements.

The main tasks of a chairperson **during** the child protection conference are to:

(i) ensure that ethical norms are observed;

(ii) keep the conference focused on its main purpose and objectives, with the child as a central focus;

(iii) elicit and acknowledge the contributions of each participant;

(iv) encourage informed and factually accurate discussion which takes account not only of current concerns and risk factors but of strengths and protective factors within and available to the family;

(v) challenge the views of participants in a constructive manner;

(vi) mediate between conflicting views and encourage negotiation;

(vii) ensure that professionals and family members are clear about expectations held by each party in relation to the other;

(viii) allow adequate time to be spent planning and negotiating realistic and acceptable future interventions and services, to be confirmed by the outcome of the comprehensive assessment;

(ix) summarise decisions, conclusions and recommendations of the conference;

(x) clarify that the conference decisions and recommendations are understood by all participants;

(xi) confirm that a key professional will co-ordinate the remainder of the assessment.

After the child protection conference, the chairperson must ensure that accurate minutes are available for circulation to all participants as early as possible. Minutes should include a summary of the discussion, the final recommendations, and the names of persons who have been given responsibility for carrying out tasks. The minutes should also record any views which conflict with the final recommendations. The chairperson must also ensure that any participants who left early, who were invited but unable to attend, or who have an active involvement in the case, are immediately informed of the decisions and recommendations.

2. Roles and Responsibilities of Child Protection Conference Participants

Notwithstanding the pivotal role of the chairperson, the quality and effectiveness of a child protection conference will depend on the **willingness and commitment of all participants,** particularly with regard to the following factors:

(i) adequate preparation;

(ii) provision of written reports which cover information about the child and parents/carers, past and present concerns, own current involvement and factually based assessment of the current situation with recommendations;

(iii) open mindedness and willingness to constructively debate conflicting views, always keeping the welfare of the child paramount;

(iv) respect for the contribution of all participants, irrespective of status or previous disagreements;

(v) sensitivity to the feelings of family members present;

(vi) acceptance of individual responsibilities and tasks and a commitment to carry them out.

3. Parents/Carers Involvement In Child Protection Conferences

In line with the principle of parental involvement which underpins these National Guidelines, a child's parents/carers should be invited to participate in child protection conferences unless there are clear contra indications.

It must be borne in mind that:

(i) parents/carers normally have more information than any professional about their child and can make valuable contributions to assessment and planning;

(ii) plans outlined at conferences are more likely to succeed if negotiated while parents/carers are present;

(iii) the experience for parents/carers of waiting outside a room while a child protection conference is in progress can be extremely distressing and unhelpful. For this reason, parents/carers should participate in the whole conference. If their presence at the whole conference is not permitted, then arrangements should be made to minimise any potential discomfort likely to be experienced by them.

(iv) parents/carers are likely to feel nervous, under scrutiny and, in some cases, hostile to the professionals present. Sensitivity and preparation are required in order to reduce tensions and facilitate useful discussion.

(v) parents/carers should be permitted to bring a support person to the child protection conference, whose identity will be clarified by the chairperson to the other participants.

(vi) the purpose of involving parents/carers in a child protection conference, as with any other participant, is to hear his or her contribution and agree conclusions and recommendations. The child protection conference should not be used as a venue for making assessments of the characters, behaviours or abilities of parents/carers, nor should parents/carers be re-interviewed or interrogated at a child protection conference.

The only circumstances which may justify exceptions to the involvement of parents/carers, or their limited exclusion, are:

- where attendance by parents/carers would not be in the best interests of the child;

- if attendance might prejudice the legal position of the parents/carers;

- whilst *sub judice* information is being discussed;

- where there is evidence that parents/carers might seriously disrupt the conference;

- if, according to medical opinion, the mental health of parents/carers is likely to be adversely affected by attending;

- where aspects of the case under discussion are the subject of a file before the Director of Public Prosecutions.

The decision to exclude parents/carers from part or all of a child protection conference may only be taken by the Child Care Manager/designate following consultation with other key participants. The reasons for full or partial exclusion must be recorded in the minutes.

4. Involvement of Children at Child Protection Conferences

Children whose care and protection is the subject of a child protection conference may be invited to attend if they have sufficient understanding and are able to express their own views. Any child attending a child protection conference should be permitted to bring an adult support person selected by him or herself and agreed by the chairperson.

The nature of the relationship between a child and his or her parents/carers and the degree of any potential conflict or intimidation which may exist between them will determine whether both attend the conference at the same time.

If a child attends a child protection conference, the chairperson must ensure that:

(i)   the child and other participants have been adequately prepared;

(ii) the venue is child-friendly;

(iii) the child knows the identity and understands the role of each participant;

(iv) the child understands, relative to his or her age and stage of development, the child protection conference process, the content of the discussion, and the implications of any report, conclusion or recommendation;

(v)   the child is not exposed to sensitive information, or unnecessary detail about any abusive or harmful incidents which may have happened to him or her;

(vi) the child is not made feel responsible for any harm (s)he has experienced, or any current risk (s)he is under.

It is the responsibility of the key worker to ensure, after a child protection conference, that the child understands the implications of any decision or recommendation made. If a child does not attend the child protection conference, his or her views should always be sought in advance and represented by one of the persons present. The response to the child's views should be reported back to the child afterwards by the person who represented him or her.

5.   Preparation for the Involvement of a Child or Parents/Carers in a Child Protection Conference

It is the responsibility of the Child Care Manager/designate to ensure that training and preparation of staff should precede the implementation of any policy to involve children or parents/carers at child protection conferences. The protocol operated in each area should specify who is responsible for preparing and looking after the interests of parents/carers and children who attend. Preparation prior to child protection conferences should ensure that:

(i)   families are assisted with transport, child minding, etc. to facilitate their attendance;

(ii) the purpose and aims of the conference are clearly explained;

(iii) the venue is accessible with adequate waiting facilities for families;

(iv) procedures and protocol involved are explained;

(v)   the family is told in advance about the identity and role of each person who is going to be present;

(vi) written reports are shared with the family in advance;

(vii) the family is introduced to the chairperson in advance as well as any participants whom they have not already met.

During the child protection conference:

   (i) the chairperson must ensure that the family has an opportunity to contribute its views and to challenge those of other participants if they wish;

   (ii) participants must understand the impact that the child protection conference process may have on the child or parents/carers and act with due sensitivity. If a child or parents/carers becomes upset, the child protection conference may adjourn for a brief period.

   (iii) if a family member becomes disruptive or displays aggression, the child protection conference may be adjourned and reconvened without the child or parents/carers present.

   (iv) the chairperson must ensure that the child or parents/carers understand the implications of any decisions or recommendations.

Professionals should always be informed when children or parents/carers are going to be present at child protection conferences. Any professional who has a concern about the involvement of parents/carers should contact the chairperson in advance for guidance.

6. Child Protection Conference for an Alleged Abuser in Peer Abuse Cases

The following should be considered at the initial child protection conference:

   (i) what is known about the alleged abuser;

   (ii) the family circumstances;

   (iii) the offence committed;

   (iv) the alleged abuser(s) understanding of the offence;

   (v) the need for further work;

   (vi) any opportunity to begin work pending the legal process;

   (vii) arrangements for accommodation;

   (viii) education, where applicable;

   (ix) supervision in the short-term pending a comprehensive assessment;

   (x) family reaction to allegation;

   (xi) support services needed by child and family.

On completion of the comprehensive assessment, the child protection conference should be reconvened and the alleged abuser should be offered treatment (taking account of the legal and welfare processes) to address both his/her therapeutic needs and control and management.

7. Family Group Conferences

A model of family involvement in child protection conferences, sometimes known as the 'family group conference' or the 'New Zealand model', is now practised in some health board areas. Family Group Conferences are attended by families, extended family members and persons of significance to the child. They normally last longer than traditional child protection conferences and are comprised of different stages, normally beginning with an outline of concerns by professionals who then withdraw, leaving families to discuss the concerns and make plans and recommendations before a final session where future action is agreed between families and professionals. Areas adopting this model must ensure that adequate resources, preparation and training are in place, and that established protocols are observed at all times.

Appendix 7 *The Child Protection Notification System*

1. A child's name should only be submitted for Notification purposes following a preliminary assessment. In order to consider notifying a Child Care Manager/designate of suspected or potential abuse to a child, the person initiating the Notification should review whether there is evidence to suggest that there are either one or more identifiable incidents which could be described as abuse. There may be acts of omission or commission in relation to the vulnerability of a child, and these acts may result in physical, sexual, emotional or neglectful abuse of a child. It is important to attempt to at least review the initial information available prior to submitting a written Notification to the Child Care Manager/designate.

   It may also be possible that at the point of referral and/or Notification there is sufficient information to suggest an investigation can conclude a substantial risk of abuse or that abuse in itself has been confirmed. This may happen by way of medical/forensic evidence and/or a witness to the alleged incident of abuse, or whereby the adult perpetrator admits the risk of abuse to a child.

2. This report will be reviewed by a Child Protection Notification Management Meeting, (convened by Child Care Manager/designate) usually consisting of an inter-disciplinary group of Managers who will at very close intervals review all reports of children at risk and advise on relevant early interventions/assessment practices necessary. Subsequently, as more information may become available through on-going assessment and further quarterly reviews, a Notification Report may also be the subject of a Child Protection Case Conference or other similar inter-agency planning meetings with a view to formulating a Child Protection Plan.

3. It will be important to review the on-going Notification status of all reports and it will be necessary to consider and establish as far as possible the cause of abuse or risk of abuse and whether this report could apply to other children living in the same household. Once the Inter-disciplinary Management Review Group has reviewed a Notification Report, it will be necessary to record the discussion of this Review Group and the Recommendations for further assessment and interventions that ought to be provided to the child and family.

4. The Terms to be used for Notification of abuse are:

   (i) Suspected

   (ii) Confirmed (This may be equated with "actual"; it means either proven or admitted).

In some instances, it may be necessary to specify more than one of the above terms in relation to a particular form or forms of abuse. These details need to be accurately recorded on the Child Protection Notification Form. It may equally be possible that a particular child is referred for Notification purposes more than once in any one year. It is recommended that the identification number given to this child on the first notification remains with this child but that subsequent notifications are given either a sub-letter or a number to indicate repeat notification within the same year.

5. The parent/carer, other relevant agencies and where appropriate the child should be informed when his or her name is notified to the Board.

6. When a child previously notified in another Health Board moves into the area, his name should be notified immediately to the Child Care Manager/designate pending an initial Child Protection Case Conference in the new area.

7. In some circumstances, the Health Board will place a child in its care in a geographical area covered by another Health Board. If the child is subject to a Protection Plan, his name must be formally notified to the Child Care Manager/designate for the area in which the child is placed. The responsibility for the formulation of the Protection Plan will remain with the Health Board in whose care the child is, although close liaison between the two Health Boards will be essential.

Management of the Child Protection Notification System

8. The Child Protection Notification System should be established and maintained by the Health Board. It is the specific responsibility of the Child Care Manager/designate. It should be held securely and separately from other records. It should be administered by an experienced officer with knowledge and skill in this area (the "**designated officer**"). Information about how to access the Notification System should be available to all agencies concerned.

9. Any changes in information relating to a notified child should be referred to a child's allocated Social Worker who in turn will inform the designated officer with responsibility for the Child Protection Notification System i.e. the Child Care Manager/designate.

10. Notification Systems which are computerised should satisfy data protection requirements and appropriate steps should be taken to prevent unauthorised access and ensure the confidentiality of the Child Protection Notification System.

11. It is the responsibility of the Child Care Manager/designate to ensure that:

(1) child protection notifications are managed and maintained in such a way as to provide adequate information to appropriate professionals who may seek relevant information about a child and

(2) child protection notifications are maintained in such a way as to facilitate the provision of statistical information to appropriate sources

Access to the Child Protection Notification System

12.   There needs to be a facility to allow for a 24 hour access to all Child Protection Notification Reports. Health Boards should take steps to ensure that all relevant services and agencies are provided with up to date information about the arrangements for access and include this information in their procedural handbooks.

13.   Health Board should have agreed which professional groups require access, and procedures for confirming the identities of persons making enquiries. The professional groups to be given access to Reports may include registered medical practitioners, senior nurses, social workers, garda officers who have been designated and senior staff in the probation and welfare service. Health Boards may amend this list in the light of local circumstances and experience.

Enquiries to the Child Protection Notification System

14.   If the child's name is on the Child Protection Notification System record when an enquiry is made, the name of the key worker for the case should be given to the enquirer. If the child's name is not on the Child Protection Notification System record but there is another child on the record at the same address, the enquirer should be told of this and given the key worker's name. The relevant co-ordinator should be informed of all enquiries made to the Child Protection Notification System.

15.   Access to information on the Child Protection Notification System should only be for persons with a bona fide reason for such information and a call back system should be used to verify applications if necessary.

16.   A record should be kept of any children not on the Child Protection Notification System about whom enquiries are made, and of any advice given. If the enquiry is repeated a child protection investigation should be considered.

Children and Families Who Move

17.   When a notified child moves to another health board area, the designated officer should telephone his opposite number in that health board and confirm the information in writing. The other designated officer should ensure that the child is notified in the new health board at once, pending a case conference there. The designated officer should also be responsible for directing other services and agencies to transfer records when a family/child moves to another area.

18.   If a notified child moves to Great Britain or elsewhere, the appropriate Social Services Authority should be informed. (See **Appendix Nine**).

19. Some families in which children are abused change address frequently. There is a real danger that such children may fall through the safety net. The Child Care Manager/designate should be responsible for instigating immediate action to trace families who are missing and whose names are on the Child Protection Notification System.

Appendix 8 *Health Board Notification Form*

Copy sent to (please tick as appropriate):
SSW ( ) SWTL ( ) Sup PHN ( ) S.C1.Psy ( ) SAMO ( )

CHILD PROTECTION NOTIFICATION FORM

Please send to relevant Health Board Child Care Manager in an envelope clearly marked
PRIVATE & CONFIDENTIAL

Details of child

Name   M ( )   F ( ) D.O.B.   / / Age _____

Address: _____

Tel No.   School _____

Additional information _____

_____

Nature of child protection concerns (if more than one, please prioritise 1,2,3)

	Physical abuse	Sexual abuse	Emotional abuse	Neglect
Suspected	( )	( )	( )	( )
Confirmed	( )	( )	( )	( )

NOTE: (1) If other children in this family are at risk/subject to the same type of abuse, please tick in Household Composition (Same Concern/) below.

(2) If other children in this family are at risk/subject to a different type of abuse, a separate form must be completed in respect of each child.

Household composition

Name	Relationship to child	DOB	Same Concern?	Additional Information
			( )	
			( )	
			( )	
			( )	
			( )	
			( )	
			( )	
			( )	

FOR OFFICE USE ONLY

C.C. Area	DED	ID No.
Gardaí Notified	Yes[ ]	Date – / – / –
Acknowledgement to Reporter	Yes[ ]	Date – / – /–

Legal Custody of Child/ren

Held by (please tick): Both Parents [ ] Father [ ] Mother only [ ] Health Board [ ]

Other (please specify) [ ] _____

Is family aware of notification? Yes [ ] No [ ] If Yes, what is their attitude?

Professional Network/People/Agencies involved with family

	Name	Tel No
G.P.		
P.H.N.		
Social Worker		

Details of Reporter
Reporter requested confidentiality? Yes [ ] (please tick)

Name	Tel No
Relationship to child(ren)/family	

Details of Child Protection Concerns

Action taken by you and any recommendations for further action
Location of child(ren) now?   Any concerns re same?

Details of person(s) causing concern

Name   M [ ] F [ ] Age   Relationship to Child

Address

Signed _____   Profession _____

Date _____ / _____ / _____   Tel No _____

Appendix 9 *The Transfer of Information on Children in Need of Care and Protection when Families Move from One Jurisdiction to another*

This appendix describes current procedures by which information is transferred between jurisdictions.

1   Northern Ireland

1.1   Children who move to Northern Ireland or arrive from Northern Ireland

By an agreement made in 1996 all notifications are sent:

(i) direct from the health board to the relevant Northern Ireland Trust;

(ii) direct from the Northern Ireland Trust to the relevant health board;

The Northern Ireland Trust addresses have been circulated to all health boards.

2   England, Scotland and Wales

The Department of Health and Children regularly receives a copy of the *"List of Custodians of Child Protection Registers in England and Wales"* from the DHSS in London. The List of Custodians is circulated by the Department of Health and Children to all health boards for information.

2.1   Children who move to England, Scotland or Wales

(i) If the family move to **England or Wales** and *the location is known*, the health board should send the information direct to the local Social Service Department Register Custodian at the address given in the DHSS List. If the move is to **Scotland** the health board should inform the Child Care Division at the following address:

> Child Care Division,
> Social Work Services Group,
> The Scottish Office,
> James Craig Walk,
> Edinburgh EH1 3BA. Scotland.

(ii) If the location in **England, Scotland or Wales** is *not known*, the health board should ask to have the Register Custodians notified in England, Scotland and Wales by writing to the following address:

> The Child Protection Policy Co-ordinator,
> Social Care Group 3A,
> The Department of Health, Wellington House,
> 133-155 Waterloo Road,
> London, SE1 8UG. England.

2.2 Children arriving in <u>Ireland</u> from England, Scotland or Wales

The Custodian List advises Social Service Departments to send information to the following address:

> Child Care Policy Unit,
> Department of Health and Children,
> Hawkins House,
> Hawkins Street, Dublin 2.

This information is re-directed to the appropriate Programme Managers in all health boards for circulation at local level.

3 International

3.1 Children Moving Abroad

Information received from the **International Social Service (ISS)** on children who are in need of care and protection who come to Ireland from abroad is channelled through the ISS Correspondent c/o the A/Director, Social Services Inspectorate, located as an interim measure at the following address:

> Child Care Policy Unit,
> Department of Health and Children,
> Hawkins House,
> Hawkins Street, Dublin 2.

This information is then re-directed to the relevant health board.

Appendix 10 *Recommended Reading*

Bridge Child Care Consultancy Service (1995) *Paul: Death through neglect.* Islington Area Child Protection Committee.

Buckley, H., Skehill, C. and O'Sullivan, E., (1997) *Child Protection Practices in Ireland: A Case Study.* Dublin: Oak Tree Press.

Cleaver, H. and Freeman, P. (1995), *Parental Perspectives in Cases of Suspected Child Abuse,* London: HMSO.

Corby, B. (1998) *Managing Child Sexual Abuse Cases.* London: Jessica Kingsley.

Daniel, B., Wassel, S. and Gilligan, R. (1999) *Child Development for Child Care and Protection Workers,* London: Jessica Kingsley.

Dartington Social Research Unit (1995) *Child Protection: Messages from Research.* London: HMSO.

Department of Health (1994) *Shaping a healthier future: a strategy for effective healthcare in the 1990s.* Dublin: Stationery Office.

Department of Health (1996) *Report of the enquiry into the operation of Madonna House.* Dublin: Government Publications.

Department of Health (1996) *Putting Children First: Discussion Document on Mandatory Reporting.* Dublin: Department of Health.

Department of Health (1997) *Putting Children First: Promoting and Protecting the Rights of Children.* Dublin: Department of Health.

Dubowitz, H. (1999) (ed.) *Neglected Children: Research, Practice and Policy.* Thousand Oaks: Sage.

Farmer, E. and Owen, M. (1995), *Child Protection Practice: Private Risks and Public Remedies,* London: HMSO.

Ferguson, H. and McNamara, T. (1996) (eds.) *Protecting Irish Children: Investigation, Protection and Welfare,* Dublin: Institute of Public Administration.

Giardino, A, Christian, C and Giardino, E. (1997) *A Practical Guide to the Evaluation of Child Physical Abuse and Neglect,* Thousand Oaks: Sage.

Gibbons, J., Conroy, S. and Bell, C. (1995), *Operating the Child Protection System,* London: HMSO.

Gilligan, R. and Chapman, R. (1997) *Developing Good Practice in the Conduct of Child Protection Case Conferences: An Action Research Project.* Cork: Southern Health Board.

Hallett, C. (1995), *Interagency Coordination in Child Protection,* London: HMSO.

Irish Catholic Bishop's Advisory Committee on Child Sexual Abuse by Priests and Religious (1996) *Child Sexual Abuse: Framework for a Church Response.* Dublin: Veritas.

McGuinness, C. (1993) *The Report of the Kilkenny Incest Investigation.* Dublin: Government Publications.

McKeown, K. and Gilligan, R. (1991) "Child Sexual Abuse in the Eastern Health Board Region of Ireland in 1988: An Analysis of 512 Confirmed Cases", *The Economic and Social Review,* Volume 22, Number 2, January, pp.101-134.

North Western Health Board (1998) *West of Ireland Farmer Case: Report of the Review Panel.* Manorhamilton: North Western Health Board.

Owen, H. and Pritchard, J. (1993) *Good Practice in Child Protection: A Manual for Professionals,* London: Jessica Kingsley.

Stevenson, O. (1998) *Child Neglect: Issues and Dilemmas.* London: Blackwell.

Sharland, E., Seal, H., Croucher, M. Aldgate, J., and Jones, D. (1996) *Professional Intervention in Child Sexual Abuse.* London: HMSO.

Task Force on the Travelling Community (1995) *Report of the Task Force on the Travelling Community,* Dublin: Stationery Office.

Thoburn, J., Lewis, A. and Shemmings, D. (1995) *Paternalism or Partnership? Family Involvement in the Child Protection Process,* London: HMSO.

Thompson, R. (1995) *Preventing Child Maltreatment Through Social Support,* Thousand Oaks: Sage.

Ward. P. (1997) *The Child Care Act 1991,* Dublin: Round Hall Sweet & Maxwell.

Western Health Board (1996), *Kelly — a Child is Dead.* Interim Report of the Joint Committee on the Family, Dublin: Government Publications Office.